MINDSETS

∞

MINDSETS

∞

Susan Smith Nash

*t*P
Texture Press
2017

Texture Press
1108 Westbrooke Terrace
Norman, OK 73072
www .texturepress.org

Executive Editor: Susan Smith Nash, Ph.D.
Associate Editor: Valerie Fox, Ph.D.
Publicity / Public Relations Manager: Arlene Ang

For ordering information,
please visit the Texture Press website at
www .texturepress.org

Book design by Arlene Ang

ISBN-13: 978-1-945784-04-0
ISBN-10: 1-945784-04-0

• TABLE OF CONTENTS •

Section 3: Uncomfortable Connections –
Communities of Chance and Choice

Section 4: Inventing Ethnicity

Section 7: Exploring Your Own Mindsets

Introduction

MINDSETS is a series of brief responses to autobiographical writings by people from all walks of life and from many different perspectives. Their stories are often raw and unsettling, but they always make one reflect back on one's own life and experiences.

The idea of mindsets is to explore different points of view to engage in transformational thinking and then to model and implement successful attitudes.

Writing is seen as an opportunity for self-discovery, a pathway into understanding society and one's role in it, a way to build academic and personal success, an approach to creative problem solving, and finally, an empowering and uplifting experience.

- Diverse, thought-provoking autobiographical writings

- Autobiographical writings of "canonical" writers whom instructors know well (and whose other literary works they have taught, read, and conducted research on)

- The underlying idea is to illustrate the mindsets of individuals who are in a quest to understand themselves and their world(s). Ultimately, the writers are successful, and the writing process itself is a key to their success.

- A focus on success; individuals dealing honestly with difficult issues and situations; their stories give readers affirmation and hope

- Modeling transformational thinking, and the opening of minds to be truly inclusive

- Provocative, thought-provoking readings which inspire and encourage self respect, which in turn engenders enhanced self- efficacy

- Facilitates successful writing – through every phase from invention to revision, with individual and collaborative projects, and with unique flowchart approach

We live in a time of fake news, fake websites, and proliferations of false, misleading, and downright duplicitous information which is promulgated by social media and taken to heart by human beings who are, as it turns out in this technological, roboticized world, more emotionally fragile than ever before.

Perhaps that is why the authenticity of autobiography and life writing is so compelling. Unfortunately, the elaboration does not end with fake news. Fake lives also exist, with highly embroidered lives or life stories.

But, let's not talk about fake news or fake lives here. Let's talk about the real lives that are brought into existence by means of inspiration, determination, and the desire to put thoughts down and thus preserve for the future the quirky, individual, and utterly idiosyncratic life that is and was lived. Life writing provides a way to preserve one's own experience of life, and also to forge a connection to the lives of others.

What is most fascinating about life writing is not what people might think it is. Grand, heroic, epic actions are not what compel people to read. It is the unique ability of life writing to establish connections both emotional and experiential.

Here are a few of the attributes of life writing that cause one to feel connections:

1. **A glimpse of a mindset:** What is one's worldview? What are the prevailing values and shaping philosophies that inform one's way of viewing the world? It's useful to read the works of others and then see ourselves reflected in them (or the obverse, which would suggest we are not what we think we are).

2. **Private thoughts, internal landscapes:** Sometimes the most automatic thoughts and feelings are the most revelatory. I like to think of James Joyce in Finnegan's Wake, and Marcel Proust in A la recherché du temps perdu. The free associations that incorporate spontaneous thoughts, juxtapositions, and raw means of expression (even an invented language) have a rare authenticity and they have the capacity to awaken our own mind's eye.

3. **Responses to life events often shared by many others:** There are ceremonies and life events that most of us have experienced. We've all experienced a childhood, and thus many "firsts" – first day of school, peak event at a sport, culminating moment after a long journey (emotional, intellectual or physical), graduations. And then, there are those other bittersweet collections of events: marriage, weddings, funerals, graduations, holidays, family vacations, divorce, loss, great surprises. Not only is it interesting to make a connection through a similar event, we can also gain insight into other cultures. How

does a wedding in Beira, Mozambique, differ from one in Midland, Texas?

In choosing the life writing to include in Mindsets, I tried to find people in different situations, writing from diverse vantage points, and facing challenges and opportunities.

It would be interesting to read memoirs of people whose activities have been extraordinarily disruptive. But, those types usually use ghost writers in order to frame their narrative in heroic terms.

That is not to say I'm completely content with the range of authors. A part of me would like to include fiction that contains emotional honesty that one rarely sees in an autobiography or memoir.

Narratives of madness and secrets and dark intentions:

Dostoyevsky – Notes from Underground. We have the opportunity to fall into the thrall of a blissfully unreliable narrator. His voice is raw and honest, even if what he says can't be supported by the events.

Wilkie Collins – Armadale. Lydia Gwilt is the anti-heroine of Wilkie Collins's 1864–1866 novel, Armadale. She is a brilliant woman driven by diverse desires, crushed by her addiction to laudanum, and simply brilliantly bad. She is a conflicted soul—while she is duplicitous, even murderous, she lives and loves passionately. Her inner dialogue captured in her diary entries is fascinating.

Mary Elizabeth Braddon – Lady Audley's Secret, Dead Man's Shoes, and others. The antiheroines of Mary Elizabeth Braddon are strong and they will do anything – anything! – to obtain what they want, even if it means poisoning (or being accused of poisoning) someone. They are characters that seem well-rounded and believable – often more believable that is the case of actual life writing.

Vladimir Nabokov – Lolita. A famously unreliable narrator, Humbert Humbert takes us down a narrative pathway that if we take it literally, we are truly horrified. However, if we take it as something utterly ironic, tongue-in-cheek, and a constructed reality that is absolutely unreal and unreliable, it's a dizzying liberation of narrative, which in turn gives us permission to take flight with our own flights of words and weird obsessions.

Stream of Consciousness A la Proust / Joyce

Proust begins Swann's Way, the first installment of A Recherché du Temps Perdú, with a contemplation of sleeping and waking up and not knowing where one is, at least in those seconds before one is fully awake.

I'm instantly connected to my own life, which figures large in my own consciousness, but is pretty insignificant in the overall scheme of things.

I would say "utterly" insignificant except if I were to say that, I would be tempted to shirk my responsibilities with my family. So, I can't say my existence means nothing at all – in fact, I'm probably not the one to judge. That would be measured in things I can't completely control, but which I can at least maintain a decent attitude and follow up. I can help where I can. I can listen where I can. What is the significance? Who knows.

And, if I think that I need to measure my significance by the fruits of my labors, that's not always an easy calculation, either. There are many authors who had little or no reknown in their lifetimes, but later, because extremely influential. Here are a few:

Emily Dickinson: Emily was more or less a recluse. Her letters were (unfortunately) destroyed by her family members. But, thankfully, her very innovative minimalist poetry survived. It's amazing how her influence flowers and then wilts. When a collection of her poetry was published that reproduced the spacing exactly as she had written the poems, she received a great deal of attention. The timing could not have been better. She was rediscovered at a time when the influence of the late 19th century and early 20th century symbolists, minimalists, and innovative writers and artists were being recast as important innovators, and their work meshed with theories that were dominant (post- Marxism, structuralism, postmodernism, deconstructivism, etc.). She was championed by the dominant thinkers of the day. Whether her work was truly enjoyed and embraced for its own merits, or because it was appropriated by a literary ideology is probably not knowable. It's not likely that she would ever be a part of a grassroots popular movement or popular culture. But, being the darling of a certain group in the rarified (or once rarified) air of academe is better than complete invisibility. You need a champion.

My "mindset response" to Proust:
Traveling gives me the opportunity to disorient myself and not know where I am, or if my perceptions are valid or not. The moments (delicious for being rather rare) when I'm in suspended consciousness and do not know what where I am, are rare treasures. I can take a moment to recognize that I'm disorienting myself, detaching part of my cognitive anchor and letting my small boat drift free to the place where I am not quite sure where I am. It's like swimming in the ocean when the waves are a high and you go out farther than you should. Your view of the beach and land is blocked by the waves and you realize you're not quite sure which direction to go, and as you try to orient yourself, a current could be taking you out farther from the shore. I've had that experience a few times and it makes me respect the ocean and also my nascent hubris that creeps into my cognitive processes whether or not I'm aware of it or not.

What do you trust? Your instincts? Do you pray and ask for guidance? Do you look for signs? Not just the land but in the sky (clouds shaped like an arrow showing you the way? Celestial breadcrumbs?)

Trusting the "signs" you detect in the world around you can be an act of faith or a symptom of a severe mental illness. In the early 2000s, there were two wonderful television shows (which did not last long, unfortunately) which featured adolescents / young women who suddenly started encountering messages from a divine order that could not be ignored.

In Joan of Arcadia, the protagonist, Joan, started to be addressed by random strangers who appeared to be manifestations of God, and who told her to do things, or get involved. She resisted but eventually was forced to follow the edicts, which always set off a chain of events that materially influenced a person (usually unknown) in a very positive way. Hallucinations? Visions? Whatever was happening was deeply disturbing to Joan, and yet she was forced to follow.

In Wonderfalls (2004) the protagonist is a slacker who works in a gift store at the edge of Niagara Falls. One day, the stuffed animals, postcards, velvet paintings—anything with a face and a mouth, started to talk to her. They would not stop until she agreed to obey their commands. Thankfully, the animals were not "Son of Sam" level and did not command her to do anything violent. But, the commands were often very odd, even disconcerting.

Do we ever feel confused? Do we look for signs? Do we read meaning into the patterns we detect? I am probably not alone in saying "yes," even though my rational mind says I should not. But— a deep abiding and often irrational conviction is probably at the heart of most heroic acts and artistic (and commercial) successes. I don't know.

A Dive Into the Deep a la Dostoyevsky

And that's a great segue to Dostoyevsky, whose "Notes from the Underground" trace the madness of an individual whose tedious, bureaucratic life takes him into a world of fears, paranoias, jealousies, and a mental incarceration all the more painful for the juxtaposition of his life with the glittering aristocracy.

Dostoyevsky was writing in the 19th century in Tsarist Russia. In the next century, Mikhail Bulgakov wrote about the terrible consequences of petty-minded bureaucracies. Heart of a Dog features a bureaucrat whose soul is suddenly transfigured in a magic "switch"—a beaten, half-starved, primitive dog inhabits the soul of the bureaucrat, with quite hilarious results. In addition to questioning what it means to be human (and our animal natures), the novel is a powerful critique of repressive governments and the kinds of work that emerges in socialist technocracies such as in pre WWII Soviet Union.

Personally, I love exploring mindsets that include the irrational—whether due to magical thinking (or mental illness) or due to one's irrepressible Id (the "deep dog" in all of us).

The Apocalyptic Narrative: The Mindset Gift that Keeps on Giving

The world is going to the dogs – or worse – it's about to be destroyed for the perversity, sin, and general intransigence of its inhabitants. The world will be destroyed. Who will destroy it? Sometimes it's the hand of God, but more often, it's the natural consequence and culmination of a series of actions and attitudes. In other words, we do it to ourselves.

Is there hope? The same voice that describes the horror is the one the details your salvation. If you believe – really believe – and follow his (usually a man, but not always) ideas and directives, you'll live. In fact, you'll not only live, but you'll be privy to the secrets of the "New Heaven and New Earth."

Each time we think we've dodged an apocalyptic bullet (Cold War, Y2K, North Korea menacing California), another crops up. Now not only the messianic leader is describing the final conflagration, but also multiple "fake news" sites (once simply referred to as "disinformation") and quickly embraced by the messianic leader for use in his/her arsenal of persuasive "push points."

If the apocalyptic narrative were simply a cautionary tale, it would be one thing. But, what is most disturbing is the fact that it's clearly something more powerful because it inspires behavior. Unfortunately, it's not usually behavior aimed at changing anything, or ameliorating situations. For example, the idea that we may drown in a world that returns to its warm, watery primordial stew origins after accelerated global warming and the melting of all the polar ice and mountain glaciers has not as yet stopped the progress of deforestation in of tropical rainforests or the diminution of carbon footprints. In fact, it only seems to have served to point fingers at emissions (the industrial world), while giving a pass to the poor polluters and those who deforest and desertify their once vegetation-covered lands.

The world's peoples are fairly helpless. It's a matter of changing course based on leaders – but, are the leaders really in control? And, if so, which leaders? When we live in a world of paranoid suspicions about our political leaders, and we suspect that the puppetmasters are shadowy bankers and captains of industry, then we may feel even more helpless.

The apocalyptic leader, with his/her messianic presence and message of drama and hope, is one who is looked to as one who will true shelter from a storm of our own making.

The price for protection is high. Basically, it's everything.

The messianic leader will offer you hope, but not only do you have to believe, you generally have to make great sacrifices. You must turn over your free will, your resources, your abilities and talents, and most of all your time. Sometimes you're asked to make the ultimate sacrifice and participate in a mass suicide. But, that usually only happens when the apocalyptic leader, the mad messiah or charismatic voice, realizes that the game is up, and that there is no way out. Rather than face humiliation and open defeat, he decides to go out in a blaze of glory. But, not alone, of course. His faithful flock must go out with him. It will be the final testimony of his power and perhaps an affirmation (in his own mind) that he got as close to being an incarnate deity as is possible. Perhaps he truly believed that he would not die permanently. Perhaps he believed he would be transported to a livable space on the Hale- Bopp comet.

And, speaking of the Heaven's Gate tragedy, and the followers who donned their identical track shoes and track outfits, castrated themselves (I'm assuming there were no women in the group) and calmly ate their poison-laced Jell-O, how do we know that their souls were NOT transported to the Hale-Bopp comet? How do we know that they did NOT transmigrate somewhere in the universe?

The things we cannot yet measure are things that we cannot actually prove or disprove, except for philosophical tricks of logic, a talent that seems to have slowly slipped away from us since the time of Peter Abelard and his beloved Heloise.

Is it any coincidence that I thought of the Heaven's Gate doomsday cult in the same stream of though as Peter Abelard? I refer yet again to the interesting ways in which our minds make connections, and where and why we persist with conspiracies and magical thinking. In fact, we'll probably always prefer magic (both Glenda "good witch" types and the more traditional scary destructive Shiva-type energies which deliver to us the kinds of vengeance that make us feel we perhaps will never feel bad feelings ever, ever again).

The apocalyptic narrative is one of the most powerful and persistent narratives that exists in our world of discourse.

Apocalypse is not just about fear, destruction, and a desperate quest for self-preservation. It's also about the long-overdue destruction of forms and structures that no longer serve us well. Let's not forget that the destruction is followed by the creation of the "New Heaven and the New Earth." In other words, it's paradise.

Is it possible to get a piece of the pie – live in the New Heaven and New Earth – without doing anything? The apocalyptic narrative would suggest that the answer is a resounding NO. You have to earn your way into the good stuff. That's precisely where the danger is.

I like to think of the apocalyptic narrative as being Dionysian (as opposed to Apollonian) using Nietzsche's formulation which he set out in his first major work, *The Birth of Tragedy*. The Dionysian is characterized by flow, festivals, inebriate energy, destruction followed by procreation. In certain ways, it's not unlike Freud's notion of Thanatos (destructive urge which exists as a counterpart of libido).

However the Dionysian is also profoundly irrational, emotional, and impossible to reason with. It is diametrically opposed to the Apollonian, which is civilized, rational, calm, reasonable, symmetrical. Welcome to the Dionysian, all about ragged, howling yet self-generating urge.

If I am to say something meaningful about the mindset of the apocalyptic narrative, I can't do it without asserting clearly and without ambiguity or hesitation, that the roots of the apocalyptic narrative are in the irrational, the emotional, and the most reptilian aspects of our brains (the limbic system). So, if you start to hear the voice of reason in the speeches or pronouncements of a leader, rest assured that the apocalyptic narrative will lose its power. In order to inspire people to act—and to go as far as to poison themselves with purple Kool-Aid or to castrate themselves before ingesting poison Jell-O pudding – the narrative has to be as raw, emotional, and reptilian as possible.

When the conspiracy theorists speak of "Reptilian Aliens" perhaps they have a point. If there are such creatures, they would certainly be effective if they speak directly to our reptilian brains, and we, in our limbic system biological imperatives, can only respond with the four F's: Fight, Flight, Fornicate, and Feed.

I'm going to go grab a sandwich.

SECTION 1:

PERSONAL WRITING THAT REFLECTS A FORMATION OF AN INDIVIDUAL SENSE OF SELF

Holiday, Billie. "From *Lady Sings the Blues*," *The Norton Book of Women's Lives*. Ed. Phyllis Rose. NY: Norton, 199x: 402-405.

The headnotes suggest that most of what Billie Holiday reported about herself, and which she allowed to be published as autobiography, is invention – a myth that Billie wove about herself, with very unclear motives. This brings to mind the self-constructions of Marilyn Monroe and other people who attained celebrity in large part because they were able to invent themselves within the bounds of a cultural narrative that, on some level empowered them. According to Billie Holiday, she was born in Baltimore (not true – she was born in Philadelphia), her mother was 13 when she was born (not true, she was 19), and her parents lived together as husband and wife. Holiday claims to have been a call girl, have scrubbed steps, and worked as a maid before working as a chanteuse in nightclubs. Was she wishing to suggest that she, like F. Scott Fitzgerald's Great Gatsby, "arose from a platonic conception of herself"? Certainly there are ironies there – the Great Gatsby was a white male, and he had, in theory, access to privilege and the society of entitlement. Billie Holiday suffered from the most cruel physical and emotional cruelties of apartheid America. Was her self-invention a way of protecting herself? Perhaps the invented story is less interesting than the fact that it was invented. Perhaps it is the act itself – of invention – of spinning a tale Scheherezade-like to survive – that matters. In this case, the self is an invention constructed for the occasion of writing. It may not have much relation to how one perceives oneself in the world. If anything, it is a way to affirm the validity of one's ideas or fantasies.

McCarthy, Mary. "Yonder Peasant, Who Is He?" *Memories of a Catholic Girlhood*. 29-53.

Mary McCarthy, was orphaned along with her siblings at a young age, and adopted by miserly relatives who, although wealthy, begrudged their expenditures on the children's behalf. Her descriptions of early childhood are painful. She and her siblings are depicted as "dismal, ill clad, and unhealthy" – and ironically, their appearance simply reinforced the impression that they were waifs wavering on the edge of invisibility and/or existence. According to McCarthy, the children looked like miserable wretches, and as orphans, or charity cases, all the glory went to their benefactors for having given the children a place to live. The children were considered a burden. The children were made into objects, exploited for the aggrandizement of the privileged. Mary McCarthy exposes the self-interest in "charity" and "good works."

She also shows, in very unsentimental ways, the terrible tragedy of a family that has lost both parents to influenza, and the way the story of their death is transmitted from the grandmother to the children. From this context, McCarthy had to construct a sense of self, and the memories constituted the very texture of identity. Mary and her siblings "begged her for more of these mortuary reminiscences as we might have begged for candy, and since ordinarily we not only had no candy but were permitted no friendships, no movies, and little reading beyond what our teachers prescribed for us, and were kept in quarantine, like carriers of social contagion, among the rhubarb plants of our neglected yard, these memories doled out by our grandmother became our secret treasures; we never spike of them to each other but hoarded them, each against the rest, in the miserly fastnesses of hearts." Obviously, one has to wonder what happened to the notion of love? What happens to children who grow up with an absence of love, or who consider themselves to be a burden? Does this affect one's sense of self? Does one's core identity start to carry with it a reservoir of rage and pain, the overt expression absolutely not allowed?

Hogan, Linda. "The Snake People," *Dwellings*. 135-143.

The author is a member of the Chickasaw tribe, relocated to southern Oklahoma. The snake became a symbol for the Chickasaws – not only of the underworld, but of the people themselves. Hogan recounts her experiences with snakes in Oklahoma – most are killed, regardless of whether or not they are venomous. This is a clear analogy to the world's treatment of all indigenous peoples, in particular the Chickasaws.

For the Chickasaws, the snake is more than a symbol, a literary devise, or metaphor. For Hogan, the snakes are people – "I call them people. That's what they are. They have been here inhabiting the same dens for tens of thousands of generations, threading between rocks, stretching in the sun, disappearing into the grass. They belong here." Sometimes it is easier to understand oneself by studying what one is not. The process by which one becomes a self and the progress to self- awareness occur in the writing about it. Writing allows the aspects of one thing to be attached to another. Art does this as well. Writing is more effective, though, because the boundaries are more fluid, and it is left to the reader's imagination to envision the expression of it.

Welty, Eudora. "Finding a Voice," *One Writer's Beginnings*. 73-104.

In this chapter, Welty describes how she comes to know her characters and herself through writing. She "begins with the particular, never the general." Later, she comes to realize that the characters she creates are, or at least, contain, aspects of herself. Perhaps this is not self-evident; it would be rather shallow, even effete, if it were. Instead, the characters she creates begin to take on a life of their own, and they evolve and grow as though they were fed from a rich, inexhaustible underground spring. Of course, they are. The wellspring is the self – inaccessible except through the process of writing about a fictional character.

DuBois, W.E.B. "Of Our Spiritual Strivings," *The Souls of Black Folk*. 7-15.

The provocative and painful question – "how does it feel to be a problem?" is all the more intense when one realizes that the author has learned to consider himself, his identity, and his impact on others around him as absolutely problematic. The author is a problem. The author realizes that his mere presence symbolizes more than one simple conflict; but a series of outrages, indignities, humiliations, and broken or unfulfilled promise. The powerful message in this is that writing allows one to articulate the nature, cause, depth of the problem. In addition, it allows one to explore the psychological processes that occur when one comes to consider oneself a "problem."

Adams, Henry. "Quincy," *The Education of Henry Adams*. 9-16.

Here we have the antithesis of a Billie Holiday self-construction, the antipode of a Marilyn Monroe or a Great Gatsby – all of whom used the Great American Fluidity to construct themselves a narrative, and identity, even a name – which they could, thanks to the great fluid, amniosis of the American womb, even pass off on the rest of the populace, as they emerge from their own self-invented birth canal. Henry Adams was, as he put it, "branded" with his name, his heritage – inescapable brandings and public self, filled with expectations and throwbacks. The cloud is one of privilege – isn't it something most people would kill for? And yet, we are tempted to recall the scions of the monarchs of Europe – their decadent ways – and one is forced to look at the interior conditions that gave rise to such playboy behavior. It is not simply money. There is perhaps the futility of it all – what can, in fact, erase the burden of a name, a set of circumstances, of BackBay Bostonians? of "old money"?

Adams' narrative is an anti-picaresque. There is no way to be "street smart" or to go through life as an Artful Dodger or a Lazarillo de Tormes, or even a character from Voltaire or Rabelais. For a person who is, first and foremost, a grandson of a President, and then descendent of a Founding Father of the country – well – what do you have? You have a person locked in, without the external possibilities of Nietzchean transformation (the Dionysian, at any rate) – it's all Apollonian. Adams' narrative reflects precisely that joyless existence – and, eventually, he views his nature as a "double nature" and learns to understand himself in a very compartmentalized way.

Momaday, N. Scott. *The Names: A Memoir.* **97-103.**

This narrative takes the form of a stream of consciousness, with self-awareness coming through the seemingly random juxtapositions of pop culture, memories, dialogue, language (an imposed language – the mother language having been expunged at birth). The fluidity of the narrative opens the world of meaning-making to creative associations and new connections. That is the good side of this. The downside is that the narrative is, first and foremost, about loss – the loss of moorings, the loss of directions, the loss of a mental map. The map was language itself – a Kiowa who cannot speak Kiowa. This is a tragic memoir. If one can name, one can, through the process of naming, begin to construct a personal language, and hence a self. Later, one can worry about things like "brandings" and "souls." First, one must exist.

Rodriguez, Richard. "Aria," *Hunger of Memory*
***The Education of Richard Rodriguez.* 11-40.**

This is the ultimate narrative about how to created a "divided self"
of Laingian proportions. It's amazing that Mr. Rodriguez did not
take up burning himself with cigarettes, or other forms of self-
mutilation which typify a person who has extreme conflicts, and two
separate voices – one for the intimate, the other for the public.
Spanish was the language of the home, of tenderness, of mother-
love, of acceptance. It was considered shameful to speak Spanish, or
at least a barrier to successful incorporation in an "anglo" life. Many
cultures and countries are bilingual, with one language spoken at
home, the other spoken in public, or for "official" business (virtually
all the colonies, including the Soviet colonies). However, it is rare for
the parents to do an about-face and restrict the use of the language
that they themselves feel most comfortable with in communicating
human emotion!! The psychological consequences are detailed by
Rodriguez as an erasure of sorts; but even more as a deliberate
isolation in which he becomes an island in and to himself. His
loneliness, isolation, and hunger for the expression and reception of
love are painful to witness. It brings to mind Mary McCarthy's
narrative – she was physically orphaned, whereas Rodriguez suffers
a psychological orphaning. The question is; how does one start to
reconstruct a functioning self after such a profound abandonment?

Plath, Sylvia. "15 July 1957-21 August 1957," *The Unabridged Journals of Sylvia Plath.* **284-290.**

Sylvia Plath Biography:
http://stinfwww .informatik.uni-
leipzig.de/~beckmann/plath.html

Perhaps the most telling passages in this set of journals revolve around Sylvia Plath's deep need to write. She writes "the central need of my nature [is] to be articulate" ... "if I am not writing ... my imagination stops, blocks up, chokes me" **"I will write until I begin to speak my deep self***" (p. 286)* Plath, who is best-known for her poetry and short novel, *The Bell Jar,* and for her suicide, which was followed by attempts by her husband, Ted Hughes, to suppress the publication of some work, rearrange others. Long vilified by her admirers as the true cause of Plath's suicide, one finds a different story in her journals. In the voluminous writings, one gains insight into a maddeningly perfectionistic soul, whose conflicts with her mother and ideas about the father who died when she was young, are dealt with in agonizing detail. One sees first that Plath is brilliant and her ways of thinking are unconventional. Her life and times make her very existence problematic – what is she to do as a young woman, locked by societal constraints into profound conflicts of interest? She writes herself alive. Perhaps that is what is most valuable in the journals – the absolute affirmation that it is, in fact, possible to "write oneself alive."

SECTION 2:

FAMILY MATTERS –
FAMILY
AND
THE INDIVIDUAL MINDSET

Introduction

This section examines how one's idea of family influences attitudes, values, approaches toward life, and, above all, a sense of personal identity. Often, the identity formed in one's birth family, or in pre-teen years is one that one seeks to erase in later years. Alternatively, a family-based sense of identity which was formed in one's early years becomes the unattainable nirvana to which one gravitates, regardless of whether or not it is, in reality, a nostalgia-based pseudo-reality.

In these readings, one can see that the family can be many things to many people. For those who perceive themselves to have been marginalized or out-grouped by social class, ethnicity, or race, the family was often an island of tranquility and a refuge from a hostile world. At the same time, it functioned as an inescapable reminder that one was different from the outside world. In that case, the refuge was also a ghetto. This is not to say that all poor and out-grouped individuals had sheltered family lives. The contrary is most often true, and when the family heads of households proved to be too fragile, too flawed, too isolated to provide true protection, the children who survived did so by creating their own protected worlds, often in the realm of the imagination.For others, far from being a refuge, the family is a prison. Certainly, the walls of the prison may be attractive. The family may seem, from the outside, to be living out the American Dream.

However, the family may a prison for those laboring under unrealistic and/or perfectionist expectations of the parents. Likewise, the American Dream façade can conceal abuse, emotional abandonment, manipulation, lies and secrets. For individuals living in this setting in their formative years, the cognitive dissonance set up between the "perfect life" put on display for outside observers, and the cruelty and/or neglect within often causes one to doubt one's own perceptions. To put it bluntly: if you are told what you are seeing is not what you are seeing, and what you are feeling is not what you are feeling, how are you to trust your senses?

Again, writing is often the survival strategy of choice.

Allison, Dorothy. *Two or Three Things I Know for Sure*. 1-21.

Dorothy Allison begins her narrative with a meta-narrative, which is to say that her story about herself is all about how one constructs a story about oneself. She freely admits that story-telling gives her license to embroider and embellish. It gives her the courage to accept what might otherwise be an embarrassing past or heritage. It gives her the freedom to envision a new way of pulling together what may seem to be unrelated experiences and occurrences. More than anything, story- telling forges connections between individuals. Allison, who writes of being born into a working class family, examines the beliefs and underlying values. What makes the working class unique? What was her experience with other women in her family? What did she observe them doing? What did they value? Allison defends the humanity of individuals all too often dismissed or overlooked, and she suggests that in the absence of material things, the family tends to focus more on human relationships and interdependencies. She defines "working class" as an attitude and a set of values that emphasize family closeness, communication (through story-telling or simple conversation).

People in the working class work to live, rather than live to work. Of course, Allison does not represent all writers. Other writers suggest the working class lives too close to the edge of poverty, and such awareness makes them fearful, since poverty dehumanizes and tears apart family bonds by making it necessary to think only of survival. In the universe that Allison constructs through her story-telling, individuals gain knowledge, courage, and human values because their working class values encourage them to have tight-knit family values, and love. It's enough make everyone want to move to rural South Carolina, rent a trailer home in the country, and work at the local WalMart. Let me tell you THAT story!

Morris, Mary. *Nothing to Declare Memoirs of a Woman Traveling Alone.* 229-236.

By traveling alone, Mary Morris escapes the limitations that her own culture has imposed on her because of her gender and her out-of-mainstream values. Of course, she steps right into another culture's values, which can be more restrictive than one's own. But, in this narrative of escape, Morris sidesteps such traps. She is considered the absolute outsider, and thus given a bit more flexibility in her dealings with individuals. Being an outsider means, also, that people can mess with her with impunity. They do so. But a travel narrative is also a quest narrative, and Morris is shaking off the chains of cultural expectations in order to invent herself or to be able to reconfigure her own ability to perceive the phenomenal world. In southern Mexico, Morris observes the culture and her own responses and reactions to it. This is very prosaic, even scientific, until she falls ill. After that happens, all bets are off. She could die, and the reader knows it. The mystery of "difference" rises up and surrounds her, and the ideas, symbols, and new ways of interpreting the world that have surround her are unleashed in her unconscious mind. She dreams. The reader can observe that she has been given the kind of vision that is given to those who go deep into the jungle and stay there until they see the image of an animal or bird, which will take on deep symbolic portent as time goes on. In this case, her visions led to actions that saved her life. The travel narrative emphasizes that it can be of immense value to move beyond the comfort zone of family and familiarity.

Jen, Gish. "What Means Switch," *Growing Up Asian American*. Ed. Maria Hong. 235-254.

By moving in the 1960s into the predominantly Jewish community of Scarsdale, New York, Gish's family becomes an island in and to itself, while the children gain a better appreciation of what they are by being surrounded by what they are NOT. What does this essay reveal about Gish's mindset? There is a certain amount of Schadenfreude at work here – the malicious glee that one derives from playing games, and tricking people through their own misconceptions and misperceptions. Instead of feeling she needs to educate her neighbors and classmates in what it means to be Asian-American, Gish takes delight in deliberately obfuscating the truth about herself and masking herself with cliché and stereotype. The funniest moments in the narrative occur when another Asian joins her school. Although he is Japanese and she is Chinese, and the two nationalities are historical enemies, she never bothers to illuminate the situation to her companions. Instead, she plays along with their wrong-headed beliefs, and uses the situation to her advantage. In Gish's case, the family is a refuge – a place where she can go and laugh at the jokes played on the outside world. It also gives her a chance to accept her difference as an advantage, and to learn to see the doors of possibility that it opens. Such a mental exercise foregrounds the author's own prejudices and values, which leads to self-awareness. For Gish to be able to toy with the prejudices of those around her, she was required to look very closely at the values and attitudes of the various groups of people around her. Although it is an excellent analytical approach, the downside is that one starts developing an "us" and "them" approach, and attitudes begin to harden.

Walton, Sam. "Raising a Family," *Made in America My Story*. 86-99.

Honestly! Why not entitle this book *Self-Reliance* and be done with it?

The narrative, along with the beliefs and values embodied here are the direct descendents of Ralph Waldo Emerson's famous essay, "Self-Reliance" (1841). These are the ideas and words that shaped an entire nation's sense of self, and they perfectly embody the core values of independence, autonomy, individuality, and belief in oneself. Emerson, who was a part of the American Transcendentalist school of writers, which included Whitman and Thoreau. What is not said is perhaps more interesting than what is said. True to American Transcendentalist thought, Sam Walton talks about the value of developing a dream, creating of an image of it, and then taking the steps necessary to actualize the dream. He does not think of himself as an individual – instead, he individualizes the family, and makes them an extension of his personal dream and his vision.

The fact that he succeeded with his dream vindicates him. If he had not been successful, how would we view his activities? What if he had been a compulsive gambler? Certainly, his children worried that he was too much of a risk-taker. What if he had packed up his children, hitched the homemade trailer to the car, and wedged vacation between visits to his business ventures? He may have seemed negligent, with child endangerment charges looming over him, rather than visionary and rich. Another aspect of Walton's narrative reveals that his story is told from the vantage point of privilege. He assumes that his primary struggle or dialectic is with himself. His life-struggle involves taming and disciplining the self. External factors are fairly irrelevant. Contrast this with the narrative of someone such as Richard Wright, or Henry Adams, who realize that the baggage of what they look like or where they were born always precedes them. Walton's "heartland upbringing" and his "bedrock values" are commendable; but they only operate in that way when conditions are perfect. His mindset would have been quite different if conditions had not been quite the same.

Brooks, Gwendolyn. "The Mother," *Black Voices*. 461- 462.

This has to be the ultimate "family narrative" being that it is the narrative of regret and of what might have been. There is a bit of horror involved as well – Brooks' poem approaches the subject of a woman who reflects back on abortion. The abortion is not merely physical; it refers to an existential condition as well – that of aborted dreams, of twisted, mutilated, and physically extracted hope. It echoes Langston Hughes' "dream deferred" but brings the horror inside, into the deepest and most life-giving reaches of the body.

Wright, Richard. *Black Boy*. 32-43.

Wright's childhood is an image, upside-down and reversed, of the children of Sam Walton. They were compelled to work. They felt nervous about their fate – sealed as it was, by the actions and attitudes of their caretakers. They had fewer choices in life than people around them assumed they had. Nevertheless, their experiences are far different, perhaps because Wright's situation as a black young man in a poor neighborhood during segregation forced him to consider the external world's assessment of him before he could even begin to assess, or know, himself. Thus, his idea of himself grew out of other people's attitudes and opinions. In contrast, Walton's children were taught that what the rest of the world thought mattered less than what they thought of themselves. Their goal in life was to decide what it was they wanted out of life, not how to placate the raging beasts around them long enough to stave off death. One notices immediately that Sam Walton operates from the point of view that "the world is his oyster." He doesn't worry about whether or not the cops will be called because he pulled into town with his homemade trailer at an hour when the sun is going down. Before speaking, Walton does not have to look at other people to see how they are looking at him. He assumes that the innate "rightness" of his thoughts and ideals will carry him through the day.

In contrast, Wright operates from the point of view of assumed powerlessness. He realizes that he must overcome prejudice and misinformation before he can make a point. In order to even consider "self-actualization" Wright must first have secure footing from which to make his first step. This is a long time in coming. He must reprogram himself so that he does not automatically censor himself, or limit his goals because of internalized feelings of worthlessness, or self- immolating rage. It may be impossible for a

Sam Walton to appreciate the inner landscape of Richard Wright — 80% of the work that Richard Wright must do in order to arrive at the self-actualization stage may have been handed to Walton on a silver platter, simply by virtue of the fact that he was born white, middle-class, and in a time of an expanding economy.

Eastman, Charles A. "An Indian Boy's Training," *Indian Boyhood*. 41-50.

There is no such thing as the "nuclear family" in Charles Eastman's community. The concept of "extended family" is a bit vexed as well. The focus of childrearing is the passing along of the mindset that is considered to be the most aligned with the values held by the community. From the very beginning, the mother is assumed to have the ability to influence the disposition and thought processes of her unborn child. For that reason, she closely controlled her contacts and her moods. What this suggests is an underlying sense of responsibility – not only for oneself, but for the actual physical welfare of others. The sense of responsibility extends beyond mother and child, but incorporates uncles and aunts, who think carefully about the way they seek to influence the way the child learns to perceive the world. The roles are clearly spelled out – courageous, adept at hunting, a quick- witted warrior. Instead of focusing on self-reliance, the tribe emphasizes interdependence and interconnectedness. The connections are assumed to be there, even if one cannot see them in the world of phenomena and superficial appearances. This is absolutely critical to the understanding of this mindset versus that of person born into a family that stresses independence, autonomy, and an ability to disconnect, even disregard others as though human beings were self-contained units.

Martinez, Ruben. *Crossing Over*. 238-249.

Here, as in Charles Eastman's Indian boyhood, family unity is considered to be a cornerstone of survival. There is a remarkable ability to pull together and endure what others would consider to be unbearable conformity, verging on a communal existence that does not reward individual prowess, solitary entrepreneurship, or even the romantic "loner" persona. For example, the Enriquez family lives together in one house, sharing what their typical middle-class American neighbors consider to be tight quarters, with three even four people per bedroom. Instead of insisting upon privacy and separate accounts, the family members pool resources. They drive together in a communally owned vehicle, and when they receive their paychecks, regardless of the amount they have earned, they contribute the entire amount to a common family fund. They pay the basic living expenses, and then divide the remainder equally. One wonders if the high wage earners will eventually begin to resent the "slackers" or if the low wage earners will be uninspired to progress, since the rewards are the same, regardless of effort.

One can see that the Enriquez family is developing a mindset that is, in large part, a response to the lifting of limits, both emotional and economic, that constrained them in Mexico. This seems to be most definitely the case for the women, who are able to dress with more freedom in the U.S. and not have to wear the traditional "rebozo" that connotes modesty and family limits. Further, they are able to purchase labor-saving utensils and appliances that make their domestic sphere a great deal more bearable. One notes immediately that the "freedom" that the women enjoy comes with a price. With their ability to work outside the home comes the reality of a never-ending day. Their workday is followed by another workday at home while the men relax. In addition, the women are more open and speak of male abuses in ways they never could at home. In many ways, life in the U.S. does seem like a little paradise, and it puts a new perspective on the notion of the American Dream.

While for someone like Sam Walton, the "American Dream" denotes economic opportunity, for Mexican immigrant women, it means a chance to have choices. The choices may seem ludicrously basic to a white, middle-class second or more generation American, but it is often not easy to grasp how survival and interdependencies in a working class Mexican family often precluded such choices. There are trade-offs – needless to say, the tight-knit fabric of the Mexican family will be stretched or even torn as the family members tend to go their own ways. Nevertheless, there is a great deal to be learned by understanding the mindset that accompanies a family willing to make sacrifices for the survival of the whole.

SECTION 3:

UNCOMFORTABLE CONNECTIONS – COMMUNITIES OF CHANCE AND CHOICE

Introduction

Often, what you have in common with other people is what you hate most about yourself. Often, the group you are placed into is precisely the group you are seeking to escape. Often, the people you have the most intense love-hate relationship with are the ones you cannot survive without.

Why does life have these little ironies? Can you think of these situations in your own life? What causes them? Perhaps they spring from the fact that our early lives are typified by external classification, grouping, and caretaking arrangements. Convenience and necessity are determinants. Usually, it's not your convenience they're talking about. They're talking about their own convenience, and their own needs. And who are "they"? They are members of your "community" who are, for better or worse, at least temporarily connected to you in ways you may not even be able to see clearly.

This is a good time to define "community."

Liu, Eric. "The Chinatown Idea," *The Accidental Asian*. 86-96.

Eric Liu writes about his Mandarin-speaking grandmother from mainland China, affectionately referred to as Po-Po, who lives in Chinatown, although she does not speak Cantonese and does not have many points of contact with her neighbors, who are from Hong Kong. Outsiders tend to look at Chinatown as a monolithic whole, and are not able to differentiate between the real, the staged, the natural clustering of like-minded individuals, and the accidental juxtaposition of people who have only vague connections with each other. As in the case with many of these readings, the "community" members have only the slightest connection with each other, and the labels attached to them are created by others because it seems convenient or because they anticipate commercial gain.

Liu sees a parallel between Chinatown and the Amish community he visited as a young boy. In both cases, there is a commodification of difference; and ethnicity has become a product that is packaged and sold in tours, on travel brochures, and in media outlets. The very look, feel, and essence of the "ethnic experience" are determined by consumers, who tend to be not of the community itself. After a time, the outside community (mainstream or consumers) exert a normative effect on the ethnic community. They unconsciously reinforce the practices and sights that are comfortable to them, while rejecting or forcing change on the ones that are not so picturesque or convenient. Eventually, false drives out the good or the real because the false image is often more palatable to mainstream audiences. One thinks of the Disney version of *Pocahontas* and the fact that schoolchildren not only believe the Disney version, they prefer it and refuse to accept the historical facts. To put it in post-colonial terms, one consequence of the commodifying gaze is enforced alterity. If you look at something as though it is a thing or an experienced to be consumed, you will always view the thing as somehow different, removed, or "other" than yourself.

Eric Liu mentions an encounter with a counterpart -- a young Amish boy, who seems to him to be already dead, or at least his fate predetermined by the desires of others to preserve a certain myth. The cultural artifact – be it an Amish community or the idea of Chinatown – is preserved for the satisfaction of the Other. The inhabitants are prisoners of it. In the case of Po-Po, her individual dreams and aspirations are so masked by the layers of imposed cultural artifact that any surfacing of it results in a response that is something between shocked disbelief and denial.

Didion, Joan. "On Morality," *Slouching Towards Bethlehem*. 157-163.

Didion examines commonly held ideas about what is moral and what is not moral. Shared ideas of morality are what create communities, and the ongoing dialogue and debate are the community's "glue."

Didion responds to a man who witnessed a fatal car accident and later comment that "you can't just leave a body on the highway – it's immoral." What makes it immoral? She reflects that her own community of people of shared "morality" possess a common upbringing. "We are what we learned as children," she writes. She heard "graphic litanies of the grief awaiting those who failed in their loyalties to each other," which illuminates the man's behavior. Does he refuse to leave a body because to do so would violate the code of behavior that allows him to be a part of a community? Didion's discussion poses a question: Is his behavior a demonstration of an absolute moral code, or is it something that evolves over time, within a specific group of individuals, in response to survival needs?

Didion is deeply suspicious of the idea that morality can be individually constructed, or that one person has exclusive access to a divine authority. She asks "how many madmen have said, 'I followed my own conscience?'" She also points out that many murderers have justified their acts by positing their own moral credo. For Didion, morality and conscience must be, at least in part, controlled or regulated by the community, and they are most effective when collective. Nevertheless, one always has the freedom to question. Didion's essay may raise more questions than it answers; and perhaps that is the point. If she were to answer all the questions and put the issue of morality to rest, would she herself be one of those self-deluding megalomaniacs who claim to have insight that no one else possesses? The purpose of this writing is to provoke thought and discussion – precisely the type of discussion that helps create community "glue."

Wolfe, Thomas. "Asheville Times, May 4, 1930," *Thomas Wolfe Interviewed 1929-1938*. Ed. Aldo P. Magi and Richard Walser. 5-11.

Wolfe maintains, rather disingenuously, that he was surprised when *Look Homeward, Angel,* the novel he wrote from a small garrett in New York City about a North Carolina community incited anger, suspicion, and a sense of betrayal. He defended his portrayal of the town and its citizens: "the people in my novel were real people to me and I loved them." Nevertheless, he broke ranks when he wrote about them and interjected his own opinion and his own value judgment. This provides excellent insight into the way that a community views itself. It is not acceptable for the individual assessment of a place to override the collective. What makes this autobiographical novel a rather uncomfortable read for the members of the community is that it is utterly human, and it predates the confessional genre of writing made famous by writers such as John Berriman, Maxine Kumin, Sylvia Plath, and Anne Sexton. Wolfe, who died at age 38 from tuberculosis that resulted in tumor-like brain tuberculomae, which resulted in progressive weakness and a massive seizure following surgery, wrote voluminously. One of his most famous novels, *You Can't Go Home Again,* was published after his death.

In this interview, Wolfe examines the idea of writing about a community and the response by the community itself. He suggests that the best way to write it is to not be drab or dull, but to write with passion for life, and to capture the characters, the unique settings, and the concrete details that make the place uniquely itself.

O'Connor, Flannery. "To A." *Letters of Flannery O'Connor: The Habit of Being*. Ed. Sally Fitzgerald. 97- 122.

Notice how people write when they are writing letters rather than memoirs. When they write to another person, certain assumptions are made. These include the following:

1. The two who are writing – both writer and receiver – share a common language;

2. They share experiences, and the letter refers back to shared experiences;

3. They have a mutual understanding of underlying beliefs and/or values, and even if they disagree with each other, the understanding of what these beliefs are is something they have in common;

4. The writer and receiver are familiar with the same people, and the people they refer to are important to each for more or less the same reasons;

5. The writer and receiver tend to read the same things, and they share the same ideas about what is considered legitimate knowledge.

The shared assumptions make meaningful personal letter-writing possible. They also are what enable one to create a community. To an outside reader, and not the recipient of her correspondence, Flannery O'Connor may seem dogmatic and her Catholic faith very rigid. However, when one realizes that her medical condition is grave, and that she is suffering from the lupus that will eventually kill her, albeit slowly and painfully, her vehemence against what she considers "nihilism" touches the reader on another level. It is not simply a diatribe against the existentialist philosophy that was so popular at the time of this letter, and which undergirded so many of the important works of literature. Her letter communicates the core of the values that inform her short stories and novels. She has an aversion to move toward nothingness, and she refuses to accept that individuals can or should create their own code of behavior. She also rejects a notion of the ultimate meaninglessness of existence. Perhaps her argument seems grounded in the post-WWII milieu. However, given the proliferation of apocalyptic narratives in the late 20th and early 21st centuries, perhaps this concern is more timely than ever.

It is a search for meaning. In the search for meaning, one must look at antecedents and influences. For O'Connor, this is at the center of her meaning-making process, and it involves reading, thinking, and discussing with friends. Reading and thinking create substance. They build a world that has structure and sequence. As she writes, she writes her world into existence, and thus partially overcomes nihilism. The activity also allows her to forge life-sustaining communities, even though she cannot be physically with the people she has chosen to be part of that group. The connections she forges both make meaning and give her a way to overcome the pain and physical isolation that are consequences of her condition.

For O'Connor, the world rests on certain absolutes, and an idea that truth, goodness, and morality are inviolable, unmalleable precepts. If one can only discover what they are, one will be able to rest upon a firm and unshakeable foundation. Always suspicious of those who reject the lessons of history and the canonical notions of life, truth, justice, and knowledge, O'Connor loves to probe that dialectic in her fiction. She creates characters who are profoundly deluded, either by their need to be important, or by their rejection of their heritage (their family, their religion). Hazel Motes in *Wise Blood*, endeavors to create his own church, *The Church of Christ Without Christ*, and it results in his undoing. Similarly, Hulga, in "Good

Country People" is so assured of her own wisdom and intelligence after returning to her small country home with her Ph.D. in hand, that she is duped by a traveling Bible salesman, who steals her artificial leg and runs off. O'Connor's characters – absurd, grotesque, and immanently human – always receive their just due.

Anaya, Rudolfo. "Cuatro," *Bless Me, Ultima.* 39-45.

Although the story is about the lessons imparted by Ultima, a curandera or healer, to a young boy, Antonio, it has several levels of signification. For one, it is a narrative that deals with healing the essential rifts and divisions within oneself. In *Bless Me, Ultima,* the rifts are assumed to be due to a collision of bloodlines – maternal and paternal – in a person. The clash of bloodlines is deeply symbolic of a more profound rift, and the healing of any inner divides or inner conflict. Ultima gives the young Antonio a strategy for understanding inner conflict, and for self-acceptance. She allows him to look at the various aspects of one's self and psyche as positive features and sources of life and energy, not simply conflict and discord.

Perhaps the herbs she gathers have actual healing power in and of themselves. Perhaps not. In any event, as Antonio collects herbs with Ultima, he learns a mindset that focuses itself on healing, and the steps required to heal. Here, healing becomes its own language. It is a language that digs deep into the psyche and asks the individual to be flexible enough to undergo great change and great challenge. It is also a language of integration and inclusion -- perhaps not with one's immediate community, but with those who practice traditions from the past, and who impart an awareness of hidden knowledge. For Ultima, hidden knowledge is empower knowledge, and the language of healing is the language that releases the power of icons such as the Virgin of Guadelupe. Before discounting *Bless Me, Ultima* as being too "New Age" or mystical, take a look at the role of nature, and how you perceive that healing truly takes place. If the mind has the power to facilitate healing, does it have the power to tear one down? How? Further, how would one's life change if he or she focuses on healing language rather than a language of rupture and division?

What are the first steps? Must one go on the journey alone, or is it best to go with a curandera, or healer? The guide is critical, and sometimes the writing process itself is one's guide.

Malcolm X. "Saved," *The Autobiography of Malcolm X*. Ed. Alex Haley. 195-212.

Why do people write letters to people they do not know? In contrast with Flannery O'Connor's letters, which are written to trusted friends and confidantes, Malcolm X writes to Elijah Mohammed, a person he does not know, but with whom he deeply desires to establish a connection. He has read Elijah Mohammed's work and he is gripped by the conviction that the problems facing the black community can be changed.

Although on the face of it, Flannery O'Connor's letters have very little in common with Malcolm X's letters to Elijah Mohammed, there are many similarities. Both are limited by their life situations, and are confined due to either illness or incarceration. They both need to reach beyond themselves and establish a connection with a person with whom they share values and beliefs. Needless to say, it is vital that the letter-writer share the same values as the receiver. For Flannery O'Connor, the language is that of writing, Catholicism, and philosophy. For Malcolm X, the language is that of faith, social justice, and awakenings. In both cases, a "standard" English is required in order to demonstrate to Elijah Mohammed that he shares values, they have read the same texts, and most of all, that they have had the same "lightning-bolt" type of awakening. In addition, they both write to correct or reverse prevailing views of black men. Tired of the pejorative connotations of "black," they write to posit that white is evil, and that "white devils" have created misery for people of non-white color. To white readers, this sort of letter raises concerns and does not necessarily create a bond. The white reader is likely to ask about how the Russians viewed the Ottoman Empire, or, centuries earlier, how they responded to the Gheghis Khan and the Mongols. To do so, however, misses the point of the Malcolm X / Elijah Mohammed connection. Malcolm

X is a man seeking hope, affirmation, and dignity, and he wishes to join a larger community; one which will empower rather than trapping and emasculating him, as his did his birth community.

Malcolm X writes a narrative of transformation, based on the core belief that his contact with Elijah Mohammed has led to his salvation from an almost certain doom. At the same time, it is a narrative of an awakening to the transformation that has been gradually taking place and effecting real change in one's life, probably over years. It is also a narrative of desire – a desire for connection, and a desire to be able to write in such a way that someone cares enough to respond. Perhaps this is the goal of all letter-writing. In addition to making connections, there is the development of community-building responsiveness. It takes courage to care, and it takes courage to listen (or read) in a way that is open enough to allow oneself to be touched. Somewhere in Malcolm X's road to salvation was a stretch where he could admit to himself that he was vulnerable, and could re-assess the life he had lived as a street hustler, invincible until the day he would die, preferably in a blaze of glory.

If you were to write a letter to your own personal hero or heroine, how would you begin? What would you say that would demonstrate to them that you are sincere? How would you write so that they would respond to you?

O'Connor, Flannery. "To John Lynch," *Letters of Flannery O'Connor The Habit of Being*. Ed. Sally Fitzgerald. 138-139.

Flannery O'Connor's community – one created of necessity and by fortuitous circumstance or chance – is important because it gives her the support she needs to transcend the boundaries imposed upon her by the prejudices of community or family into which she was born. She writes of the willingness to take chances with her writing and to be willing to overcome the internal censor: "I once had the feeling I would dig my mother's grave with my writing, too, but I later discovered this was vanity on m part. They are hardier than we think." O'Connor goes on to share a few more examples.

The advice and insight are invaluable. Writers and scholars should never self-censor, at least when in the initial stages. This is not to say that one should not be careful about hitting "send" after dashing off a flaming e-mail that seems (at the time) to just absolutely dazzle one with the subtle arguments and incisive commentary. That is a different issue. In writing ideas, the tendency is to be much more sensitive about one's own writing than anyone else might be. O'Connor's observation puts things into perspective. It also reminds us that what connects us to other people is writing that is honest, *about* something, and which doesn't shrink from real details or the specifics of a situation. It expresses real feeling, and thus is exemplary of true humanity. Writing from the heart, with honesty, creates a connection in the reader and lays the groundwork for a community to emerge. The community forms itself around shared experiences, beliefs, people, places, current events, thoughts, and the specific, concrete details from which new worlds can be constructed.

Kingston, Maxine Hong. "White Tigers," *The Woman Warrior*. 19-53.

Maxine Hong Kingston's narrative is built on a paradox. On the one hand, in the community she chanced to be born in as a female, girl children are considered worse that useless – they are considered to be a burden. On the other hand, the Chinese culture she chooses to identify with has a long tradition of myth and "tell-story" (as her mother puts it) about brave, valuable and valued women.

Through "tell-story" Chinese girls learn about themselves and their eventual destinies, and the way the world regards and will regard them. The irony is that the story the most memorable to the girls is the one the least likely to be realized in their lives. It is the story of the Chinese woman warrior, and here, in Kingston's narrative about herself and her consciousness, she weaves the myths together with the factual details of her life. The woman warrior fights, avenges, wins, and reverses the injustices in life. She is invincible. She possesses supernatural skills, abilities, and is admired to the point of worship. The longing to be a woman warrior is a sad counterpart to reality. In Kingston's world, and in the world of her mother and grandmothers, Chinese girls were considered worse than useless. They were considered a burden and eventually traitorous family-abandoning. All investment and accomplishments realized by the Chinese girl would simply remind her family of what she would take from them.

Kingston's narrative represents a stratagem for self- overcoming. She imagines herself alive by writing the dream. Perhaps the attributes she desires will only have life in her interior journeys, and in the development of a mental sphere that gives and breathes promise to others. Nevertheless, it is effective, as Kingston juxtaposes the dream of the warrior, who is assertive and avenging, with reality of extreme submission and the denial of needs.

The agents of change are the animals – the cranes, the white tigers, the white horses – who wield magic with their presence. The old couples and magical characters from a time long ago come into her life. They give the dreamer power, freedom, and self-actualization. The "tell-story" is what also imparts to the young girl a sense of wonder.

Are fairy tales appropriate modes for instituting real change? Kingston's narrative is ambiguous on this point. She has knowledge of who her enemies are, but how can she resist? She has "gun and knife fantasies, but did nothing useful." The warrior woman fairy tale without a correlative "other" in the phenomenal world which might give a person a way to implement the dreams is, perhaps, simply a route to resignation.

Marshall III, Joseph M. "Afterword The People," *The Lakota Way*. 206-223.

Joseph Marshall is writing what amounts to an extended definition in order to establish or re-establish what has been lost or overwritten. As a member of the group of Native Americans known as the Sioux, and divided into Lakota, Dakota, and Nakota subgroups, Marshall writes to establish an identity, and to describe to others what constitutes community, particularly one that has undergone erasure. He wishes to correct the misconception that all Native American groups are or were the same. As is the case with many Native American writers, Marshall focuses on two primary factors which both differentiate his community from others and which correct misconceptions. The first, which is language, is presented as a living artifact of a culture that once had a complex and dynamic structure, but which has been denied any possibility of true continuity. Members of a community must speak the same language. Granted, this language does not have to be a linguistically pure dialect or idiolect possessing its own distinct vocabulary and rules of grammar and syntax. Nevertheless, it does have to unite people and be capable of expressing what is unique about a set of people who share values, experiences, friends, beliefs, and life stage-commemorating ceremonies.

Further, Marshall writes to define the roles and activities of the member of his community. At first, this may not seem to have any particular importance and worse, seems almost to be an extension of a cliche. However, one begins to realize how totally the groups who invaded the Americas had stripped the Native Americans of their humanity, reducing them in the collective unconscious to "savages." Whether the "savages" were "noble" or diabolical makes little difference; the fact is that the way that Native Americans lived before times of extermination, genocide, and constant warfare has been more or less obliterated. What Marshall does is to point out that many of what are now considered to be the community's defining characteristics were responses to the barbarism of the times. For example, in war, the Sioux often did not kill each other. Their raids were intended to show valor and courage. Battles over control of territory did not require bloodshed. In contrast, the attacks by white troops were extremely bloodthirsty, and the intent was to kill as many Sioux as possible, thus reducing their ranks and making a land grab all the more viable. When a community defines itself not by competitions and displays of valor, but by forcing its youth to engage in an apocalyptic battle that means almost certain death, then the whole tenor of the community changes. Once a community views itself as doomed, and its only hope constituted of sacrifice and suicide, one wonders what kind of legacy will be left behind. What will be the prevailing values, language, and beliefs? It is good to ask these questions before it is too late.

SECTION 4:

INVENTING ETHNICITY

Introduction

This chapter deals with authors whose memoirs and writings reveal that they considered it necessary to develop a new concept of ethnicity in order for them to feel a stable sense of identity. Ethnicity itself is a problematic concept, because of the definition of it is slippery at best. According to Ugbana Ukpo, an anthropologist investigating ethnicities in Nigeria, an ethnic group is a group of people having a common language and cultural values, whose commonalities are reinforced and emphasized by frequent interaction between the people in the group. In Nigeria, the ethnic groups are occasionally fusions created by intermarriage, intermingling and/or assimilation. In such fusions, the groups of which they are composed maintain a limited individual identity .

According to *The American Heritage Book of English Usage*, "the idea of otherness, as measured by such attributes as nationality, religion, language, or race, is central to ethnicity" (*American Heritage* 1996). It is precisely the "otherness" that the writers explore. However, instead of focusing on difference in order to outgroup themselves, they focus on the process of identifying and naming an ethnicity – their own – in order to be a part of a social entity.

In this chapter, the learner will develop a working definition of ethnicity, and be able to analyze the concept as applied to individuals, society, and communities. Learners will gain an understanding of how ethnicity is constructed or invented, and will be able to explain why individuals may seek to define themselves in terms of an ethnicity. In addition, learners will understand what the group perceives as the costs and benefits of being affiliated with a group. Finally, learners will make connections between the subject and writings and their own experience, and will be able to describe the mindset(s) involved.

Themes and topics explored include the following:

- Individual senses of alienation within the dominant culture;

- When and where banding together as a group helps the individual survive;

- How the determination of ethnicity is a naming process, and how naming and labeling are similar and different;

- Who tends to apply labels and why;

- The relationship of power to naming, labeling, and ethnicity;

- The relationship of powerlessness to the motives and reasons for labeling and identifying groups;

- How poverty and labeling are toxic when combined;

- How ethnicity and labeling are combustible when combined.

Nye, Naomi Shibab. "Newcomers in a Troubled Land," *Never in a Hurry: Essays on People and Places*. 3-16.

Naomi Shihab Nye was born in St. Louis, Missouri, to an American mother and a Palestinian father. At age 14, Nye's family moved to Jerusalem, where she attended high school for one year. Later, she moved with her family back to the U.S., settling in San Antonio. As an Arab-American, Nye has been able to look at ethnicity from the vantage point of a person whose family defines its identity around a sense of loss, struggle, and renewal.

In the selection presented here, "Newcomers in a Troubled Land," Naomi Shihab Nye contemplates names and the traditions of naming in the U.S. and in the Arab community she lived in when she was 14. She thinks of her own last name and its meanings and implications. Later, when she marries, she is fascinated by her new last name. She contemplates it "with warm affection" because she is, as she puts it, "merely a tenant of this name Nye." For her, the name, Nye, is marvelously appropriate because it is derived from the Danish prefix "Nye," meaning "newcomer." She likes the concept that a last name can indicate the existence of a long-lost connection or tribe, even if the last name came into being as the invention of a creative employee at Ellis Island. As a member of the Palestinian diaspora, Nye, only half tongue-in-cheek, sets out to track the Nye diaspora, and invites everyone in the San Antonio phonebook with the last name, Nye, to dinner.

"Newcomers in a Troubled Land" (which engages a bit of wordplay and suggests "Nye's in a Troubled Land") takes place in St. Louis ("Gateway to the West") where her family settled at first, and then later, in San Antonio, where she meets her husband. Her account of settling and moving takes place against a backdrop of multiple diasporas that Naomi is able to see, due to her own background and experience.

The mindset explored here is one of mapping diaspora, and understanding ethnicity, not by country or place of origin, or by race or religion, but by the common experience of diaspora. It is important now more than ever because so many of the world's peoples share this common background.

Nye emphasizes in many ways and forms that individuals are not necessarily wedded to an "essence" or primordial sense of identity. Instead, she shows how a sense of identity evolves over time, and is often the result of ruptures and responses, and is not planned. Ethnicity is, like identity, constructed by what people perceive themselves to have in common with others. Sometimes, this is an activity rather than an attribute or characteristic.

Nye is an award-winning author of short stories, poems, and works of fiction for children.

Conley, Dalton. "Race Lessons," *Honky*. 37-52.

This is the memoir of growing up poor and white in the urban housing projects of New York City. It is important because it addresses the notion of learning how classification and determinations of race are made. According to Conley, "Learning race is like learning a language."

This selection allows the learner to see roles reversed, tables turned. The white male is now a part of the underclass. Ironically, although the author's family was as poor or poorer as their Puerto Rican, black, and Asian neighbors, the young Dalton perceived that there were advantages to being white, despite the isolation felt for being the only white in the school system. He drifted from ethnic group to ethnic group, adjusting himself to fit in. Ironically, his best "fit" was with the Asians, to the point that his mother claimed she could not immediately pick him out of a crowd of his Asian friends.

Unlike other whites, Conley did not immediately believe he was a part of an entitled race or ethnicity. However, he gradually came to believe his race caused others to respond to him with a certain amount of deference. Whether or not this was true became irrelevant. As he believed it, he became capable of taking of advantage of his situation.

This is written against a backdrop of social change and social experimentation, with desegregation, the "War on Poverty," busing, changing ideas about race and race relations. Shifts in perspectives make individuals hyperaware of how they relate to each other and the differences by which they define each other.

Conley's school is multi-racial, which does not mean the classrooms are racially mixed. Instead, the classes are divided according to ethnicity, which actually reinforces stereotypes and rigid thinking.

Ironically, it does not facilitate mutual comprehension or tolerance. Instead, what results is an awareness of how people act, dress, behave, with limited interaction. The label attached to a person is difficult to dislodge or peel away. Thus, it is difficult for people in that setting to think beyond the signs or the iconography that presumably denote an individual's essence.

The mindset explored is that of learned defensiveness. Because of the color of his skin, it is assumed that Conley and his sister enjoy the perquisites of power and privilege. Ironically, this is not true until Conley starts believing it, and starts playing the game. This selection corrects the misconception that all whites are middle-class or rich, and live in the suburbs. It also, however, suggests that no one can ever completely transcend race, as much as they might like to think that privilege is race or class-neutral.

If race is learned like a language, it is learned via social interaction. In order to transcend categorical thinking, or stereotyping, one must look at individual cases, and focus on the particular rather than the universal. Overgeneralizing and drawing conclusions based on the whole leads invariably to inequities.

Anzaldúa, Gloria. "How to Tame a Wild Tongue," *Borderlands / La Frontera: The New Mestiza.* 75-86.

In the essay, "How to Tame a Wild Tongue," Gloria Anzaldúa describes her childhood as a Chicana (Tejana) in Texas, where her sense of self was influenced by what she calls the Tejano "tradition of silence" with respect to their native Spanish language. For her, to be "Tex-Mex" is to learn to suppress one's heritage, tradition, and language. The Chicanos she refers to are inhabitants of the Valley of South Texas, who settled there from Mexico and Spain several hundred years ago. Located in the midst of a constantly shifting population of various Hispanic groups – recent immigrants from Mexico, 7th-generation Chicanos, refugees from Central America – her group is often confused by outsiders with others.

Azaldúa realizes that she needs to learn not to be ashamed of her "wild tongue" that speaks the wild and wonderful Tex-Mex Spanish which is characterized by archaisms, Spanish words reaching back to the Middle Ages, anglicized slang, uniquely Tex-Mex idiomatic expressions, with a unique accent, and a unique pronunciation. Their language marks them as a separate group, and one which predates the more prosperous newcomers, the Anglo business owners and dominant culture. She needs to learn how to be proud of her "wild tongue," and she needs to show others – especially Tejana women – how to do the same.

Anzaldúa uses language as a point of departure to show precisely how a group differentiates itself over time and eventually invents its own ethnicity. Language is one of most clear-cut markers of ethnicity. Family traditions, customs, and holidays are another.

Her mindset is one of pride of identity, one in the process of accepting the depth and complexity her own identity. In many ways, it is a process of correcting misconceptions. One of the larger misconceptions is that Chicanos – those who speak "Tex-Mex" Spanish – do not actually have an identity and that their language is not "pure" and thus not "real" when in fact it has its own syntax, vocabulary, and grammar.

Anzaldúa's essay demonstrates that language is sometimes the best access point into understanding how a group defines itself. Communities speak the same language. They also tell the same stories and follow the same traditions, even if their legitimacy is not acknowledged by the economically dominant group, or if they perceive that they have to "go underground" in order to survive. Individuals must work through a sense of inferiority or invisibility as they speak the language that seems to deny them economic access and participation in the society at large.

Hosokawa, Bill. "The Matter of Ethnicity," *Out of the Frying Pan: Reflections of a Japanese-American* 93-97.

Hosokawa, a survivor of Japanese-American internment camps in California during World War II, reflects upon the consequences of ethnicity and labels – ones that are manufactured and applied to a group and not by the group for and to itself. This is a memoir and an essay about what he perceives as why it society begins to believe it is permissible to apply racial stereotypes to some groups and not to others.

Who invents an ethnicity? Who decides which racial stereotypes are "acceptable"? When do groups appropriate the stereotype, adopt it as their own and essentially defuse it, thus transforming the racial slur into a kind of "brand image"? Is there any reason to do that, anyway?

Bill Hosokawa contemplates why Japanese sterotypes have not been adopted in the general population. He perceives that the Irish have begun to show pride in images that were once considered racial slurs, which indicates a group's belief that they have, in fact, arrived and are accepted in the culture.

Understanding that images and racial stereoptypes are invented is key. The question expands, and involves an inquiry into who invented them and for what purpose. The commodification of "otherness" is a partial explanation. The idea of making a spectacle of difference is another. This selection addresses the misconceptions that a) all racial stereotypes are created equal, so that it is acceptable to use them as the basis of humor; b) that a cultural group that appropriates its own racial stereotype is somehow empowering itself or nullifying or negating the toxicity. This is patently not true, except to say that some anti-heroes seem to suggest that it can happen.

A key life lesson in this is to remember that racial stereotypes are often ugly reminders of a painful past. For Asian-Americans, it is a past marked by virtual slavery building railroads, forced settlement in racially-delineated ghettoes (Chinatowns), exploitation for cheap labor, paranoia, and suspicion. Lingering misconceptions should be brought into the open and one should inquire why certain stereotypes, racial slurs, and hate speech persist. If one denies them, or allows them to fester unchecked, the underlying social dynamics that give rise to this will not be brought to light.

Mankiller, Wilma and Michael Wallis. "Origins," *Mankiller: A Chief and Her People*. 15-29.

Wilma Mankiller's essay traces the Cherokee people's creation story, with an emphasis on oral tradition, which suggests that groups transmit ideas about ethnicity and identity via origins-stories, even when the stories are shown to be historically problematic.

In addition to emphasizing the essentially democratic political structure of early (preColumbian) Cherokee socity, Mankiller's essay explores the regard of Cherokees for women and how this respect was reinforced by stories and oral tradition. Mankiller's narrative serves the purpose of differentiating her tribe from other indigenous tribes, and most particularly, from paternalistic Europeans.

Wilma Mankiller, chief of the Cherokee tribe, writes from the tribal center in Tahlequah, Oklahoma, established at the terminating point of the Trail of Tears. The essay is written against a backdrop of what Mankiller characterizes as Western historians' disinformation, which sought to further perpetuate negative stereotypes.

Mankiller's narrative exhibits a mindset of "setting the record straight." As she says: "Precious few non-Indian people are aware of the role native women played in ancient tribal societies." Mankiller emphatically refutes the notion that tribal women were "drudges or ethereal Indian princesses." Partially written to explain her role in the tribe and to locate it as a part of a long tradition, Mankiller's essay demonstrates how racial chauvinism reinvented an identity so that it needs to be reinvented today.

She also writes to correct the misconception that Indians were savages before the Europeans' arrival and that the Europeans somehow "rescued" them from godless chaos. Instead, Mankiller argues that the standard of living, political organization, and gender relations were highly egalitarian and democratic, with an emphasis on harmonious coexistence with nature. Mankiller's argument may be a bit self-serving, and yet it does encourage one to see things from a new point of view.

The essay demonstrates that it is vital to re-examine history and one's identity and to find out how much it was constructed by historical, political, and/or economic exigencies. It takes a long time to reverse misinformation, especially when it reinforces hierarchies already in place and certain ideas about race.

Baraka, Amiri / Jones, Leroi. *The Autobiography of Leroi Jones / Amiri Baraka.* 57-62.

Leroi Jones, who renamed himself Amiri Baraka, is an award-winning poet and writer. In this memoir, he traces the origins of the jazz- inspired poets to that of BeBop and Jazz. He describes the importance of Black musicians and African-American art forms in the development of a certain pride of origins and ethnicity, which ran counter to the dominant influences of segregated, race-defined cultures.

BeBop and jazz presented to the young LeRoi an alternative mod of self-expression and a new approach to writing – one which was not overly burdened by the past, but with acknowledged antecedents and heritages.

This selection demonstrates the conscious invention or reinvention of ethnicity through writing and creative self-expression. In this context, creative self-expression provides an avenue for growth and the affirmation, not only of self, but also of community. He primarily depicts his life in the 1950s and 60s, and his encounters with jazz musicians, all of whom played a prominent role in the development of a sense of self. Especially prominent is Charlie "Bird" Parker, who is, in many ways, a sacrificial figure. "Bird," whose playing was both expressionist and abstract, while being highly technical, was the musical counterpart of the art world, where Jackson Pollack and others explored the limits of self-expression. As was the case of early Modernism, the predominantly Euro-Caucasian art world appropriated African and African-American influences. However, for Jones, there is a significant difference. He is able to retain ownership and any appropriations do not cross race lines (although they do cross socio- economic ones.) As a black, he draws from black experience. He uses it as a way to survive and grow as a human being. Unfortunately, many of those who influenced him were not so lucky. Charlie "Bird" Parker, Billie Holiday, and others died of the consequences of drug abuse or self-destructive lifestyles. One could argue that for the pioneers, self- destruction was one of the prices that society unconsciouslessly exacted of those who dared put a voice, a sound, a story, or a message to the black experience, riddled, as it was, with pain, humiliation, and yet, through it all, hope, faith, and community.

The mindset is one of exploration and creative self-expression. He corrects the misconception that writing poetry is an isolated activity. Instead, it occurs within a particular context and setting, and it creates a community as well as an ethnicity. A valuable lesson: creative self- expression can save your life – at least for awhile (!)

Sarton, May. *The Journals of May Sarton: At Seventy*. 245-252.

May Sarton (1912-1995) was born in Belgium, but moved to England and then to the U.S. when war broke out in Europe. Although a prolific poet and novelist, it was Sarton's journal and memoirs written in her late 50s, which launched her wide-ranging popular appeal. Her solitary contemplations of the nature of work and life opened a door upon a deeply private person whose inner struggles rehumanize the often terribly isolating challenges of aging.

This selection, drawn journals written at age seventy, chronicle daily life. Her reflections on life are intimate, and the details she uses are closely rendered. As a seventy-year-old writing, she rehumanizes aging. Her "ethnicity" is an identity based on how people are most likely to categorize her. She writes in response to the misperceptions people have once they label a person. In refering to Virginia Woolf's words, she captures the driving force behind the need for self-expression: "This insatiable desire to write something before I die, this ravaging sense of the shortness and feverishness of life, makes me cling, like a limpet to my rock, to my one anchor."

Sarton's journals demonstrate that beneath every label, every invented or constructed identity, ethnicity, or label is a human being. That human being shares the essential feelings, emotions, and sensations that others do, and it creates a bond.

The mindset is that of a person who believes it is important to express one's day-to-day experiences and thoughts, and to make sense of it all, no matter how seemingly trivial. After all, meaning comes from the details.

In writing her journals, Sarton addresses and corrects misperceptions about aging and older people. She provides valuable life lessons because she maps out the points of contact, and the commonalities we all share. In reading the journal and intimate thoughts of an individual, the reader comes to see how much we all share.

Thomas, Piri. "Barroom Sociology," *Down These Mean Streets*. **169-178. "Afterword to the Thirtieth- Anniversary Edition,"** *Down These Mean Streets*. **333- 337.**

This memoir presents a tongue-in-cheek view of sociological investigation, with the fact of racial stereotypes juxtaposed against individuals attempting to transcend labels, or alternatively, transcend their own ethnicity.

Thomas' memoir shows the tragedy of the rigidity of racial classification and the fact that even if one wishes to redefine oneself, one still has to deal with the fact that people judge based on appearances. Thomas illustrates how ethnicity is not just color, tribe, race, or nationality. It also involves one's way of speaking and attitudes, cultural attitudes, language, gestures, beliefs, and fashion.

The memoir is humorous because it emphasizes the absurd. Thomas' "investigator" comes across as arrogant, self-absorbed and exceedingly blind. Brew comes across as ironic, angry, and convinced of his own impotence, except to erupt in useless and self-destructive violence. Piri sees both sides, and presents to use the big picture. We, as readers, become poignantly aware of his existential bounds and limitations.

The memoir recounts events that took place in Norfolk, Virginia, in a bar, as a man who defines himself as multi-racial (white, Malaysian, black, etc.), introduces himself as a sociologist seeking to understand the "Southern Negro." The reader gets the impression, however, that his primary objective is to differentiate himself from precisely that "Southern Black" label he seeks to understand. He wants to set himself apart, which is quite understandable. After all, this is taking place in the 1950s, during a time of high anxiety, segregation, and rigid notions about race and class.

The mindset illustrated here is one of humor – although there is a hard edge to it, as though Thomas wishes to ridicule anyone who would presume to attempt to escape the limitation of society's labels, and to reinvent and/or redefine oneself. For Thomas, the idea of "passing" is a constant undertone, as is "exposing." He also reveals the absurdity of certain racial stereotypes, in particular, the notion that the blacks living in the South somehow have learned to live with and even love their poverty, being happy-go-lucky, joyous, and earthy.

Thomas' approach can be applied to society at large. One does tend to infantilize or demonize the poor, and portray them as either incapable of complex thought or evil. Alternatively, the poor are often stereotypically viewed as somehow attuned to nature, and are shamanistic.

∙∙∙

"Definition of Ethnicity." The American Heritage Book of English Usage. 1996. http://www .bartleby .com/64/C006/031.html *accessed 7 May 2002.*

Okpu, Ugbana. *Ethnic Minority Problems in Nigerian Politics: 1960-1965.* Stockholm: LiberTryck AB, 1977.

SECTION 5:

BRAVE CHOICES – LOVE, SEXUALITY, GENDER

Introduction

This unit includes readings that will help the learner develop an awareness of the ways that individuals write about how they choose to deviate from society's norms. It also helps one understand how people experiment with their lives, or communicate with others in order to view the same issue or phenomenon from multiple points of view.

Sometimes such approaches are a matter of life or death. For Anne Sexton, who was hospitalized for depression several times, and who was characterized as a person who was so thin-skinned she seemed to have no protective layers at all, the ability to share her survival strategies with another struggling writer was important. Reading her letters heartens one, but it also underscores the essential tragedy of her life: she committed suicide in 1974. For others such as Horace Axtell, a Native American whose life was in a downward spiral after prison, choosing to learn about Native American religious practices gives new hope and meaning in life.

The readings in this section also help the reader break away from stereotypical thinking about taboos such as mental illness, and to understand how people from within that set of circumstances develop support systems. After reading the selections, the reader will be able to describe how people see a society in transition, where understanding oneself involves understanding new modes of art, expression, music, and languages.

Themes explored include what it means to be raised as a poor black girl in the segregated South, why and how modernity encourages self-annihilation, how one develops the desire to transcend socially-constructed barriers to spiritual and personal development, and how journal-writing becomes a way to develop new attitudes. Primary is the need to retrain the mind to accept oneself and to understand how respond in a productive manner to cultural, sexual, gender, and ethnic diversity.

In each of the narratives, there are moments of chaos, disorder, and unknowability. Rather than retreating from ambiguity, the narrators move forward, trusting that from chaos emerges a new order, and new configurations of self and society.

Sexton, Anne. "Flee on Your Donkey: November 1963- May 1967," *Anne Sexton A Self-Portrait in Letters*. **Ed. Linda Gray Sexton and Lois Ames. 288-297.**

Anne Sexton (1928 – 1974), a poet writing primarily in the 1960s and early 1970s, was part of the "confessional" poetry movement, which was characterized by a new openness about personal issues and life. She wrote with great frankness and candor about her struggles with mental illness, which was diagnosed at various times as depression, anxiety, mania, and bi-polar disorder. She also wrote about love, her relationship with her husband and family. Sexton was a transgressive poet, willing to write about breaking taboos. Primarily known for her poems, Sexton also wrote letters, which shed light on the thoughts, inner struggles, and turbulent emotions which inform her relationships and her artistic output. Her letters demonstrate how she was able to use what would have been a paralyzing problem for others, but for her was transformable into the raw material of art and poetics.

Her letters illustrate the mindset of a woman who resists society's pressures to reject herself for being, as she puts it, "crazy" and in and out of the "nut house." In the letter contained here, Sexton talks about how she transforms the experiences she has into something she can later shape into art. She also encourages another poet who is suffering from depression. She offers kindness and support, taking chances with her open expression of affection: "It's the kind of love letter I shouldn't write." In reaching out to her fellow writer, Sexton establishes a bond and creates the beginnings of a community.

The letters are from Anne Sexton to Philip Legler, a close friend and fellow writer. She is writing from home in the 1960s, in front of a cultural and political backdrop of chaos and disord, with protests against the Vietnam War an ongoing saga. She focuses on her struggle against mental illness in order to give her friend strength and courage: "The Thorazine is good from me. I mean it really calms me down and has more or less saved my life when it needed saving."

The mindset illustrated is that of a person engaged in a daily struggle to transform mental illness into something that gives others hope. What results is also a way to write from experience, and attempt to open up new ways to describe the human condition.

The letter corrects certain stereotypes and misconceptions about mental illness, and it re-establishes the humanity of those who are struggling with depression or bipolar disorder. She writes to Legler: "Don't worry if they say you're crazy. They said that about me and I was saner than all of them."

Sexton has both feet on the ground, and is compassionate, yet pragmatic when responding to Legler's apparent infatuation. Her discussion of love and its limits is illuminating, as she discusses their mutual love as a mirror they use to understand each other, and, most of all, themselves.

Sexton's poetry won numerous awards, including the Pulitzer Prize for *Live or Die*. Her oeuvre includes the following:

- *To Bedlam and Part Way Back*. Boston: Houghton Mifflin Co., 1960.
- *All My Pretty Ones*. Boston: Houghton Mifflin Co., 1962.
- *Selected Poems*. London: Oxford University Press, 1964. (Poems selected by Sexton from *Bedlam* and *All My Pretty Ones*)
- *Live or Die*. Boston: Houghton Mifflin Co., 1966; London: Oxford University Press, 1967.
- *Poems* (with Thomas Kinsella and Douglas Livingstone). London: Oxford University Press, 1968.

- *Love Poems*. Boston: Houghton Mifflin Co., 1969; London: Oxford University Press, 1969.
- *Transformations*. Boston: Houghton Mifflin Co., 1971; London: Oxford University Press, 1972.
- *The Book of Folly*. Boston: Houghton Mifflin Co., 1972; London: Chatto and Windus, 1974. (Poems and stories)
- *The Death Notebooks*. Boston: Houghton Mifflin Co., 1974; London: Chatto and Windus, 1975.
- *The Awful Rowing Toward God*. Boston: Houghton Mifflin Co., 1975; London: Chatto and Windus, 1977.
- *45 Mercy Street*. Edited by Linda Gray Sexton. Boston: Houghton Mifflin Co., 1976; London: Martin Secker and Warburg, 1977.
- *Words for Dr. Y.: Uncollected Poems with Three Stories*. Edited by Linda Gray Sexton. Boston: Houghton Mifflin Co., 1978.
- *The Complete Poems*. Boston: Houghton Mifflin Co., 1981.
- *Selected Poems of Anne Sexton*. Edited by Diane Wood Middlebrook and Diana Hume George. Boston: Houghton Mifflin Co., 1988.

Houston, Pam. "Cowboys Are My Weakness," *Cowboys Are My Weakness*. 108-125.

Pam Houston (b. 1962) was born in New Jersey, received a degree in English from Denison University (Ohio). Later, she entered graduate school at the University of Utah. As a licensed river guide and accomplished horsewoman, Houston writes from her life. *Cowboys Are My Weakness* is written in the first person as fiction, but as Houston puts it, "everything I write is 82% true."

The story, "Cowboys Are My Weakness," from the collection of the same name, aligns itself well with the notion of "Brave Choices," because it deals with a woman who is determined to make choices of lifestyle that counter the mainstream. She is a pioneer in a time that is suspicious of pioneers, and tends to label them cultural imperialists, colonizers of the imagination, or worse. In this story, the protagonist searches for a man whose values – love of the outdoors, the West, and general earthiness – help her express her desire for unities of earth and body. She craves the harmony and fulfillment she feels only in the outdoors. Thus, the activities of humans and animals in the outdoors function as extended metaphors for what goes on in one's quest for the perfect life.

Somewhere along the way, Houston's protagonist realizes that her ways of seeing the world have been shaped by an almost mythic conception of the American West, which encompass love, one's relationship to nature, one's own body, freedom, and the question for the "impossible love of a country song." The protagonist of the story lives in Fort Collins, Colorado, where Homer, her friend and lover, is a "wildlife specialist in charge of a whitetail deer management project" in Montana.

The mindset explored is that of a person who is examining one's own dreams and long-held ideas about love. In this examination, she has to face the fact that what she wants does not square with she does to obtain what she wants. Further, the story takes a hard look at how stereotypes tempt one to judge by appearances. What is a "real" cowboy? Further, what is a "real" anything?

Pam Houston has written numerous short stories, which have appeared in *The New York Times, Mademoiselle, Vogue,* and other magazines and journals.

hooks, bell. *Bone Black: Memoirs of Girlhood.* 7-12, 31- 47, 88-90.

Born in Hopkinsville, Kentucky in 1952, bell hooks (née Gloria Watkins) has published numerous books and articles, which explore what it means to be a black woman in America. She uses the languages of academic discourse and film/literary criticism to deconstruct art, literature, and film depictions of race and gender. Her writing has been quite controversial, even polemical for its radical feminism. *Bone Black* is a departure. It is a quiet narrative, an intimate memoir of childhood and the awakening of perception.

The selection that appears below explores how attitudes about love and marriage come to be shaped. Here, hooks writes of her reactions and responses to grade school pageants in black schools in Kentucky, one of which was a so-called "Tom Thumb Wedding" in which children dressed up for a mock wedding. According to hooks, this is one of the ways children are taught society's attitudes. As a child, she was uncomfortable with the not-so-subtle messages: a) if your parents have money, you'll get to be a bride; b) if you're a black with light skin or straight hair, you will receive preferential treatment, and perhaps get to be a bridesmaid; c) women must suffer disappointments in love in silence.

Set against a backdrop of racial segregation, intolerance, and prejudice, hooks' narrative demonstrates how firmly ideas are implanted into the consciousness of the individuals enacting pageants and dramas. In addition, it shows how one must become aware of how and what one has learned about race. Race reveals itself to be a construction rather than an absolute. Behaviors and attitudes are equally artificial, and in learning (or being taught) to "fear white folks," hooks comes to realize that she will spend much of the rest of her life unlearning these early ideas.

The narrative seeks to correct stereotypes about race and attitudes (how all "white folks" are presumed to think about blacks). It also seeks to show how vital dramatic enactments are in the educational process. For hooks, it is important to analyze enactments (pageants and drama) and images (such as in *The National Geographic)*, to see how they reveal a false consciousness, and promote negative stereotypes, deceptions, and pejorative attitudes. Further, the erroneous thinking is often inscribed onto the consciousness of impressionable children who participate in pageants, dramas, or enactments that perpetuate the myths. What hooks does is encourage introspection, analysis, and critical thinking. What is applied to the pageants she writes about can also be applied to cultural texts, films, videos, and music.

bell hooks has been a prolific writer of film, music, art, literary, and cultural criticism. Her work allows the reader a way to re-examine the world around him/her and to see the subtexts and cultural messages embedded in images, words, and song.

Lash, Joseph P. "For Life, For Death," *Eleanor and Franklin* 101-103.

Although this is an excerpt from a biography, it contains fragments from original letters, which constitute autobiography. These letters are useful because they provide insight into a political marriage and the idea that it is through a partnership, rather than a solo effort, that one's hopes and dreams might be realized.

The letters are supposed to illustrate how individuals who are in love write to each other. What it does, in fact, is illustrate how two individuals who have been trained to think of themselves as a part of a dynasty, have selected marriage and love as a duty rather than an overriding passion. Written in the early years of the 20th century, the letters comment on school, travels, obligations, and expectations for the future. They are set against a backdrop of power, family networks, and duty. It becomes very clear that decisions cannot be made without collective approval by the family, which further illustrates the dynastic view of the structure of one's life.

The mindset explored is one of privilege. If you are a part of a dynasty, you automatically think you are entitled to tutors, music lessons, travel, expensive clothing, and more. Constrast this with bell hooks' *Bone Black*. In her world, even music lessons are "earned" and in no way automatic. It is clear that she is being taught at a young age that she is somehow not as worthy as those who were born into wealth and privilege.

The selection combats the stereotype that the rich and powerful have no sense of social responsibility. In contrast, the letters between Franklin and Eleanor illustrate that duty, family obligation, and work for a higher good are primary objectives.

A lesson learned is that you *are* worthy. You must choose partnership rather than solitary effort. You must also choose commitment and a belief in the power of the tribe.

Other works by Eleanor Roosevelt include *My Day,* which is a compilation of the articles she wrote daily for publication in newspapers.

Ellison, Ralph. "Epilogue," *Invisible Man*. 559-569.

Ralph Ellison (1914 – 1994) was born in Oklahoma City, Oklahoma. His ground-breaking novel, *Invisible Man* (1952), explores the consciousness of a black American man who seeks education and opportunity in a world marked by treachery, ambition, exploitation, and erasures of self. Ellison's epilogue personalizes the novel, and creates a sort of first-person confession.

Here, Ellison's brave choices take the form of self-examination. Unlearning the lessons one has been taught, deconstruction the false arguments that keep people oppressed are life-long tasks that must constantly be renewed. Ellison describes the consequences of not simply repeating what people wanted him to say. He also delves into the difficulties that accompany honesty, and explains why and how, instead of hibernating himself away and avoiding conflict, he finally chooses to speak and to act.

The selection is written in the first person and the narrator is Ralph Ellison. It is set in the 1940s. He writes because he does not want to continue to be a "mere pawn in the futile game of 'making history.'"

The mindset illustrated is that of a person who is rebelling against conformity, hibernation, "invisibility," and conformity. Ellison writes, "Whence all this passion for conformity anyway? – diversity is the word. Let man keep his many parts and you'll have no tyrant states. Why, if they follow this conformity business, they'll end up by forcing me, an invisible man, to become white, which is not a color, but a lack of one."

Ellison writes to counter the position that it is better to conform and be silent and invisible than to speak up and voice one's opinions and/or views.

Life lessons here are valuable. As Ellison himself puts it: "Why do I write, torturing myself to put it down? Without the possibility of action, all knowledge comes to me labeled 'file and forget.'" Thus Ellison writes in order to remember. He also focuses on conceiving of a plan of living.

After the success of *Invisible Man*, Ellison was in great demand for his lectures on race relations. He planted seedlings of change, which grew and helped the nation move away from apartheid.

Fong-Torres, Ben. "Groovy Kind of Love," *The Rice Room* 130-137.

At a time when second-generation Asian-American sons were encouraged by their families to aspire to become white-collar professionals such as accountants, doctors, or lawyers, Ben Fong-Torres gravitated toward the world of rock'n'roll. He worked as a journalist and was an editor for the *Rolling Stone*, with 37 lead front-cover stories to his credit. *The Rice Room* is a memoir of his formative years.

Fong-Torres describes the difficulties of love for a second-generation Asian-American. It was impossible, at times, to find a woman who understood his "transitional identity" between generations, values, and attitudes. When he does find a woman who shares his experience, he finds that he is merely a stepping stone to more mainstream boyfriends. The mindset of second-generation Asians is complex: "we had the same feelings toward our parents, the same mix of devotion and rebellion."

The main character in this memoir is Fong-Torres himself. It takes place primarily in the San Francisco Bay area in the 1960s, against a backdrop of social protest, chaos, changing values, music, and new personal freedoms.

The mindset being explored is one of searching for connections, which includes acceptance from a girlfriend. He finds that there are problems in interracial dating, no so much between individuals, but between their families.

The narrative seeks to correct misconceptions about the meaning of interracial dating, and to counter stereotypes about how Asian-Americans think. The narrative allows a glimpse into the mind of a person who defines himself by the music in the background (which is his personal foreground because the new music – rock-'n'roll -- reinforces his core values of freedom of expression, new ways to regard life), which is always questioning authority and/or the eternal verities, and which asks him to see himself as reflected in other people's eyes.

Ben Fong-Torres' essays and articles for the *Rolling Stone* are collected in a volume entitled *Not Fade Away*.

Axtell, Horace and Margo Aragon. "Coming Back to the Indian Ways," *A Little Bit of Wisdom Conversations with a Nez Perce Elder.* **184-194.**

After his release from prison, Horace Axtell, a Native American, finds a road to personal transformation. Axtell relates how he moved gradually away from Christianity to the native religion called "Seven Drums," which sought the restoration of Native American languages, and an Indian way of worship. Song, dancing, ritual, and prayer involved personal awakenings, and they required him to relearn, or at least re- evaluate, what he had been taught was the only way to regard religion.

The story of learning a new way to worship is also a story of learning a new way to communicate. Instead of prizing individualism, the narrator returns to a collective view of decision-making, and an Indian way of life. He discusses his actions with others, and becomes more understanding with each other.

The gradual transition from an individual to a group-focused mindset is informative, and it provides an anatomy of how one becomes more sensitive and attuned to others.

Axtell's narrative reverses or at least corrects and modifies the idea that Indian worship is what is portrayed on television or in New Age bookstores. The true emphasis is not on costume or crystals, but on the eventual results of mental and spiritual transformation, which include a positive sense of self, respect for others, regard for what others are saying, gentle ways of reproof and guidance.

Life lessons abound: "In order to make things happen in a good way, you've got to think and work together." Axtell emphasizes collective thinking, with practical attitude adjustments, such as admitting when you've made a mistake. He does not believe that a "real man" is an individualistic loner, but is a part of a community. Part of being a member of the community or extended family involves learning to see the contributions of others and to honor them.

SECTION 6:

RELUCTANT OUTSIDER – CHRONICLES OF BEING CLASSIFIED PART OF THE "OUT" GROUP

Hahn, Emily. "B.Sc.," *No Hurry to Get Home*. 56-69.

In this autobiographical chapter, Hahn describes what it was like to be the first woman to be a mining engineering student at the University of Wisconsin. Hahn, who was annoyed at her family's insistence that she go to college rather than study art, explains that, in retrospect, she should have enrolled in Letters and Science, but chose mining engineering instead. It was an unusual choice in 1924. She claims it was an accident, but after reading her work, the reader wonders if that was the case. Hahn certainly loves a challenge.

Not only was Hahn an outsider in the classroom because of her gender, she was also barred from field trips, visits to mining operations, and professional societies. Hahn, who describes in detail and with great sensitivity, the feelings she had upon being ostracized, outgrouped, and subjected to stereotyping and ad hominem slurs, prevailed. She graduated in 1928, having been voted, in a final triumph, into the engineering club.

"B.Sc." illustrates quite well the issue of the "reluctant outsider" because it deals directly with the behaviors of the in-group with respect to an out-grouped person. More vitally, it explores the pain, defiance, resolve, and eventual self-overcoming required to succeed in such an environment. Short of hazing (which assumes that the person being hazed is a part of the in-group to start with, they just have to undergo a rite of passage), the actions of the in-group toward Hahn seem to be cruel, even sadistic. Fear of change, of self-examination are clearly a part of this equation. Hahn's narrative allows the reader to see not only her feelings, but also the nervous attempts at territory-protection.

Hahn continued to "accidentally" be drawn to situations and places where she would automatically be outgrouped because of her gender, race, or nationality. Traveling alone to China and other areas of Asia and Africa, Hahn was a careful observer of the way she reacts to people and situations, and how people react to her.

As a person who is immediately outgrouped because her difference from the dominant group is immediately apparent, Hahn learns how to cope and even exploit the fact that she is overly visible, and her very presence creates spectacle. Her narrative shows the reader how it is possible to transform potential or even ongoing humiliation into triumph.

"B.Sc." is part of a series of autobiographical essays collected in *No Hurry to Get Home*. In addition to writing narratives, Hahn wrote for *The New Yorker*.

Goldman, Emma. *Living My Life*. 624-641, 685-693.

In Emma Goldman's autobiographical writing, *Living My Life*, the belief that activism can bring about positive social change motivates Goldman and others to stage protests, publish radical flyers and publications, and practice civil disobedience. Advocating such causes as birth control for women, women's right to vote, child labor laws, the eight-hour workday, union organization, and free speech, Goldman lived in the maelstrom of controversy. As an émigré from Russia (b. 1869), Goldman was familiar with the European anarchist writers and movements. Her memoir sheds light on her mindset. She is a woman focused on a goal, eager to help those around her be aware for the first time of the injustices and inequities they had blinded themselves to.

Although she worked for the rights of all women, Emma Goldman was outgrouped by law enforcement and the mainstream. Her ideas were economically destabilizing (the eight-hour workday, child labor restrictions). Worse, her notions were deeply troubling to conventional society's values. By maintaining a presence outside the "in-group," Goldman could see from a unique vantage point. She did not accept conventional explanations. For example, when entering prison, the guard asked if she had any diseases, meaning sexually transmitted diseases. Explaining that she was referring to the "diseases immoral women get," the guard went on to tell Goldman that most of the women in the prison suffered from them. Goldman responded that "venereal diseases are not particular" and that many "respectable people" had them.

The events described by Goldman take place in 1917, just months after the United States entered World War I. As she is transported from New York City to the federal penitentiary for women in

Jefferson City, Missouri, Goldman interacts with guards and prison officials, and explains her views and positions. This is not a good time for Goldman to be expressing her progressive opinions – Goldman describes the paranoia and patriotism that have gripped the land, and the new laws, such as the Espionage Act, which result in false imprisonments.

The mindset that this reading explores is that of consciousness-raising. It is one that refuses to accept the surface appearances of things as the only reality. It also refuses to accept the status quo, and always attempts to see through to the attitudes' impact on all members of society, particularly the impact on the weak, defenseless, or poorly informed, who are ill-equipped to fight back.

Goldman's narrative illustrates that it takes courage to open one's eyes to what is really going on. It is not easy to assess societal attitudes, laws, and economic practices from the point of view of its impact on various groups. An example is the Espionage Act referred to by Goldman. Although the greater goal was to protect national security, the reality was that it became a tool of ill-intentioned people to trap and/or turn in enemies (and irritants), and/or eliminate competition.

Emma Goldman was a prolific writer and wrote numerous essays and pamphlets on social reform, social justice, women's rights, children's rights, free speech, and other topics.

Baldwin, James. "The Discovery of What It Means to Be an American," *Nobody Knows My Name.* 17-21.

Baldwin's autobiographical account is the narrative of a black man coming of age in the first quarter of the 20th century, a time suffused with huge changes for in society. Although there were more opportunities for education and economic access, black men also faced worsening racism, violence, and extreme prejudice.

In this selection, Baldwin discovers that once he has moved to Paris, he is able to establish friendships and relationships with Americans that were not possible in America. Musing this fact, Baldwin explains that in America, race issues still block people. Ironically, in France Baldwin is able to communicate with Americans of all races, origins, and class because their common background as expatriates attenuates all other differences.

The selection focuses on Baldwin and his experiences in Paris with fellow expatriates. After 1948, Baldwin made his home in the south of France, where he followed a tradition of many American artists and writers, who found France to be a more hospitable place for artists and writers than America. This was particularly the case in the post World War II era, when anti-Communist fears of the Cold War made innovative writing and socialist ideas dangerous. Returning to the U.S. for lecturing or teaching engagements, Baldwin's writing addressed themes of racism and homosexuality, which made him the subject of a great deal of controversy, even within the black community. Baldwin, who was both black and homosexual, found himself cut off from the dominant culture for being both black and openly gay.

In the selection included here, what characterizes Baldwin's narrative is a sense of "thrownness." "Thrownness" was first developed as a concept by the existentialist philosopher Martin Heidegger. It is "the condition of being taken more or less by surprise, hurled into an unexpected and unpredictable situation. In one sense, all human beings are thrown: they all have to find their way through the world without much in the way of practice." In Baldwin's world, there is an awareness of being thrown into a world of which one has no knowledge – of what came before birth, or what will happen after death. The thrownness contains a feeling of randomness, and thus other individuals are perceived as part of that great outgrouped mass – a condition which makes one focus on the here and now; one's existential condition.

Baldwin writes to correct the prevailing view that people are rigid and cannot transcend their teleological view of the world, and that order, once established, cannot or should not, be re-ordered. By moving to Paris, Baldwin places himself in a state of productive chaos, from which he can emerge, reinvented as the person he wants to be, and unconstrained by the ideas of his native society. However, Europe is no utopia, and it is not an Eden, freshly created and without a history. Baldwin observes, with some irony, that the palce that allows him freedom is also the place from which the slave ships and slave- trading enterprises originated. In Europe, Baldwin's history comes full circle and he is hyper-aware of this.

James Baldwin's first novel, *Go Tell It on the Mountain* (1952), is a largely autobiographical account of Baldwin's life. Baldwin's writings include essays, novels, plays, and the best-selling collection from which the selection is drawn, *Nobody Knows My Name* (1961).

Steinbeck, John. "Budd Schulberg/1972," *Conversations with John Steinbeck*. Ed. Thomas Fensch. 107-112.

Taking place shortly before his death in 1968 of arteriosclerosis, the interview published here captures the mixed emotions of a young writer who realizes that the 60s activists have begun to consider the Nobel- winning Steinbeck (b. 1902) a hawkish curmudgeon, although Steinbeck worked all his life for the rights of farm workers and social justice.

In this selection, Steinbeck encourages the interviewer to keep the faith in the writing project he has established in Watts, right around the time of the race riots. Steinbeck points out the importance of the efforts to include individuals who do not always have access, and he comments on the psychological consequences of out-grouping.

The conversations take place with a bedridden Steinbeck, who is ill with the arteriosclerosis which will eventually kill him. On the day of this interview, he and the interviewer talk for five and half hours, locating the conversations against a backdrop of social upheaval in the United States. Reflecting back upon the 1930s, Steinbeck comments that the 60s are, in many ways, more dangerous and the outcomes less certain.

This selection explores the mindset of relentless pursuit of social justice, and the mental adjustments necessary to ensure that one is willing to look beyond the group one is championing and to include others.

The interviewer comments that although Steinbeck is considered a curmudgeon and anti-progressive in the 1960s – part of the "Establishment," such stereotypes are incorrect. Further, to stereotype is to overlook what Steinbeck's continuing involvement and support of social justice throughout the 60s. For example, the same year he died, Steinbeck contributed money to support inner-city writing groups. For Steinbeck, writing is a way to build awareness of the nature of one's struggle, and its importance. In his own works, particularly in *Of Mice and Men* and *East of Eden*, the quest for justice, and the need to right the wrongs of society echo biblical narratives. Complex morality plays or extended dramas of heroism, Steinbeck's work affirms and rehumanizes.

Steinbeck suggests that to write gives one the opportunity to create one's own identity, and to establish stable ground when the world around one is on the brink of disintegration.

The recipient of numerous awards and honors, John Steinbeck is well-known for his novels, which include *Grapes of Wrath, Of Mice and Men, The Red Pony, Tortilla Flats, Cannery Row, East of Eden*. Many were made into classic films, the most recent being *Of Mice and Men* (1992), directed by Gary Sinise, and starring Sinise and John Malkovich.

Hornbach, Marya. *Wasted: Coming Back from an Addiction to Starvation.*

Wasted is a memoir written by a young woman who chronicles her teenage years, her hidden life and self-destructive tendencies, which are masked by perfectionism and an edgy relationship with her mother. Marya Hornbacher, alternatively anorexic and bulimic, described how she was hospitalized several times, her weight sinking to a low of less than 80 pounds. Theoretically a part of the dominant culture's privileged class, Hornbacher is an enigma to those who judge people by the stereotype. Far from feeling privilege or self-confidence, Hornbacher exhibits the sort of self-loathing that one comes to expect from individuals who perceive themselves as society's pariahs.

Hornbacher's eating disorder causes her to lead a double life. The binging, purging, and recovery cycles are hidden or masked, as are the obsessive exercise and ritualistic activities. She becomes an outsider to herself. The more she tries to achieve balance between the perfectionist and the chronic "shlemiel," the more frantic and self- destructive she becomes. She is angry with herself, and with her parents. The etiology of Marya's ailment remains a mystery, even to herself, despite years and years of struggle and therapy. This selection explores some of the factors that cause Marya to try anorexia, "my Big Idea, my bid for independence, identity, freedom, savior, etc."

Marya is the primary player in this selection, and the narrative takes place at home – her parents' home – while she is a teenager. The action takes place against a backdrop of middle-class prosperity, affluence, access, opportunities. The American Dream hovers over the stage. Yet, in this theater of the perfect family, something has gone terribly wrong to create such masochistic habits. The conditions are perfect for the development of an eating disorder. Perhaps in a different setting, Marya's rage would have manifested itself as an addiction to heroin, paint sniffing, or criminal behavior. It is hard to say.

The mindset is that of a person who perpetually defines herself as a part of the outgroup, who refuses to join the mainstream. Further, a part of her refuses to thrive. Her writing is an act of rebellion against the rigid rules she has set for herself. Writing allows her to escape her self-created bonds and what seems to be an incorrigible masochism.

This selection provides a glimpse inside the mind of a person who has recovered from a strange, inexplicable, and painfully slow way to die. Instead of slow suicide, one begins to see that Marya's eating disorders are a kind of *soi-disant* physical therapy. She is attempting to rehabilitate herself from anxiety.

The primary life lesson from this selection is to see how each person runs the risk of becoming an outsider to herself or himself. After self-isolating, the individual will think, act, and plan in ways that out-group her even to herself. There is no real community or ethnicity here – if anything, meeting people with the same issues would be anathema – after all, they could reveal or expose too much. Perhaps a narcissistic culture is to blame here – after all, isn't the core problem the rage against limits? Perhaps narcissism is not the correct term. Perhaps it is simply individualism taken to extremes. The American Dream is not only the possession of creature comforts. The American Dream also involves the attainment of lofty goals -- to be special and "different" and thus achieve success. What happens when a young woman realizes that her dreams are not truly attainable, even though she has been programmed to believe that they are? Do we see a ghastly inversion of a "dream deferred" and a "raisin in the sun"? What would Hornbacher be if not a "raisin in the sun"? In this case, the "wasted" fruit might be an "apple on the grass." Think of the images. No one believes in Eden, but boy do they believe in sin. Dreams deferred? Dreams despoiled. Lots of images. Hey, it might work.

Bulosan, Carlos. *America is in the Heart.* 168-173.

Carlos Bulosan, a Filipino, writes a poignant memoir of his experiences of work, love, and life in California. He is the outsider's outsider who does not feel a sense of belonging, even within certain ethnic subgroups. As a Filipino living on the margins, realizing he cannot return to the Philippines, due to violence and threats to his personal safety, Bulosan is in a precarious situation. His experience of America is that of a series of menial jobs, short-term friendships, jail, marginalization, and economic insecurity.

Bulosan describes his mindset during the first years of life in the U.S. as one of confusion and defiance. He feels himself to be voiceless and powerless, and the world around him refuses to acknowledge his viewpoint. He dislikes the labels society has put in place, and in one instance, while he is working at a restaurant in Buellton, California, he reacts: "when a Filipino and a white woman came to the restaurant to eat and were refused, I flung my apron away and attacked the headwaiter with my fists." He was fired. No one bothered to ask, however, why he erupted in anger.

Bulosan writes to inform readers of the experiences of Filipino immigrants, and the sadness that accompanies a longing for home. Bulosan believes he has a common bond with other immigrants – he describes a conversation with a French immigrant who became sad upon hearing the wind through peach trees because it reminded him of the sounds of his native Normandy.

There are life lessons to be learned in this. One of the most compelling is that bonds are remarkably difficult to forge once one considers oneself ostracized or outgrouped. Yet, it is precisely the sense of longing, nostalgia, loneliness, and the seeming randomness of one's own existence that unites individuals. Bulosan speaks to the fact that individuals can find kindred spirits and thus bond in that way.

Brandy Carolyn. "Heartbeat of the Ancestors," *Reinventing the Enemy's Language.* **Ed. Joy Harjo and Gloria Bird. 502-506.**

Carolyn Brandy, who is Cherokee, and a drummer, composer, teacher, and, mother, writes an account to reconstruct what she knows of her family and to fully understand the consequences across the generations of being forced into a role of outsider. In her own family, great damage was done as her mother was disowned by her family for marrying a Native American soldier in 1945 as the war was ending. Ironically, the father had been disowned by his own family, who were angered by his joining the "white man's army." His family, living in Oklahoma, still remembered the Trail of Tears and other incidents, and considered the U.S. government to be the enemy.

Carolyn Brandy's parents met in San Francisco, where she grew up. Her narrative is set against a backdrop of self-destructive parents (her father, although a highly decorated veteran, had drinking problems, left the family, and served time in prison), rigid attitudes, and ethnic identity confusion.

Her mindset is one that emphasizes the need to understand the consequences across generations of making people into outsiders – in the culture, in their families, and to themselves. Her story is, as she puts it, "an American story about people intermixing and secrets." It is also a story about individuals with the frightening capacity to reject and abandon when things do not go their way.

Brandy's narrative raises several interesting issues. The first involves analyzing the long-term consequences of thinking of a person as a part of a group, rather than as an individual, who should be listened to outside the confines of narrow expectations. The second involves looking at competing approaches – one of acceptance and inclusion, the other of rejection and exclusion. Perhaps there are costs and benefits to each that are not readily apparent to those involved in the negotiation; the true impact rests upon the children, and peripheral individuals who do not even have a voice in the debate.

Mori, Kyoko. "Language," *Polite Lies: On Being a Woman Caught Between Cultures.* 3-19.

Kyoko Mori lived the first twenty years of her life in Japan, which was followed by 20 years in the U.S. *Polite Lies* describes the differences that are not always on the surface, and the subtle variations that are only observable to a person who knows each culture intimately.

As a person between cultures, Mori finds herself attempting to understand one culture in terms of the other, and constantly relating one to the other. She describes how a language defines the way people can relate to each other, to the point that if they wish to break free of certain hierarchies or customary practices, they change languages. Language, and the way its grammar and syntax define the way people communicate with each other, either resists or facilitates communication, assimilation, and mutual understanding. For Mori, the conventions of language follow the conventions of a culture, and only an insider to the culture understands what is *not* being said as well as what *is* being said.

The essay contains an in-depth analysis of the way the Japanese language delimits and defines social interaction. It is assumed that the reader already understands the way that English language conventions are restrictive and/or inclusive for certain purposes. For Mori, the Japanese language is filled with mixed messages, contradictions, and deliberately obfuscatory conventional language which masks its true message.

The essay seeks to show how Japanese and the English practiced by Midwesterners in the U.S. are similarly indirect, and which are used in the service of social conventions that bear a remarkable resemblance to each other. One comes away from the essay with an increased awareness of how language creates social reality; and then how social customs empty a language of its denotative function. If the message is far outside the actual language of the communication, one must look closely at what is being said and relate it to the social context, the individuals involved, and the nonverbal communicators employed.

This essay reminds one of Bernard Rudolfsky's *The Kimono Mind*, and other books on Japanese-American linguistic and cultural patterns.

Angelou, Maya. *I Know Why the Caged Bird Sings*. 104- 119.

Maya Angelou writes a memoir about growing up in Stamps, Arkansas, in the segregated South. Her depiction is searingly honest, and it gives faces, places, and specific names and feelings to what could be viewed as the collective experience of many growing up in the South in the first 100 years after slavery was abolished in the U.S.

As black girls, Maya Angelou and others are automatically relegated to the position of being marginalized by white society. The sense of being on the outside looking in is made even more poignant and harrowing by the fact that antebellum aristocratic values of European origin are imposed on blacks. They consciously or unconsciously buy into the vocabulary and practices of elitism by embroidering knick-knacks for a dowry chest, learning the rules of etiquette involved in setting an elaborate table, and using the language of the debutante to describe one's coming of age. Such activities primarily function to reinstate *difference* as the only way of knowing each other, and reinforce the distance that exists between white women and the black women who present such a potent threat to them. To Angelou, the linguistic and social practices of the South are a cruel joke, particularly when the more typical role of a young black girl was to be a servant in a white woman's home.

The young black female is considered an outsider – an outsider who possesses little or no power. Her powerlessness is illustrated when the white woman has the power to erase and then reconstruct identity by renaming. Angelou provides an example of this in the selection printed here. She is working in a white woman's kitchen, in what Angelou characterizes as a perverse finishing school, where she learns the finer points of setting a table, etc. Her employer, Mrs.

Cullinan, is descended from Virginia plantation owners. She surrounds herself with white friends who consider themselves entitled to "culture" and to be waited on by black servants, in an ugly echo of "the good old days." The sense of the employer's power becomes ominous with the power of naming. "Margaret" is deemed too long and is shortened to "Mary." "Hallelujah" was long ago renamed "Glory" in a creepy echo of *The Battle Hymn of the Republic.*

If renaming can dehumanize, negate, invisiblize and nullify, does the act of naming have generative powers as well?

The mindset examined in this selection is one that looks closely at the way language is used to either empower or strip away entitlement or rights. Conversely, there is an awareness that one can empower oneself by naming, and it can be used for the good.

In writing about how black girls and women were subjected to nullifying linguistic and social practices in Stamps, Arkansas, Angelou also corrects the misconception that silence denotes acquiescence or agreement. The women to whom the psychological assaults are not sufficiently empowered to be able to question or counter the practices directly. Indirect rebellion seems to be their only way to resist. Thus, when Angelou considers her situation, she seeks revenge rather than rapprochement, and obtains it when she deliberately breaks a family heirloom from the old plantation in Virginia. Sadly, no one understands the message behind Angelou's gesture, so her speaking and acting out are misunderstood and worse – processed through the unknowing and unenlightened mindset of her employer.

One does see how erasures of identity are always a part of the outgrouping process. A key lesson is that the converse is possible: ingrouping and inclusion are possible when one names oneself into it.

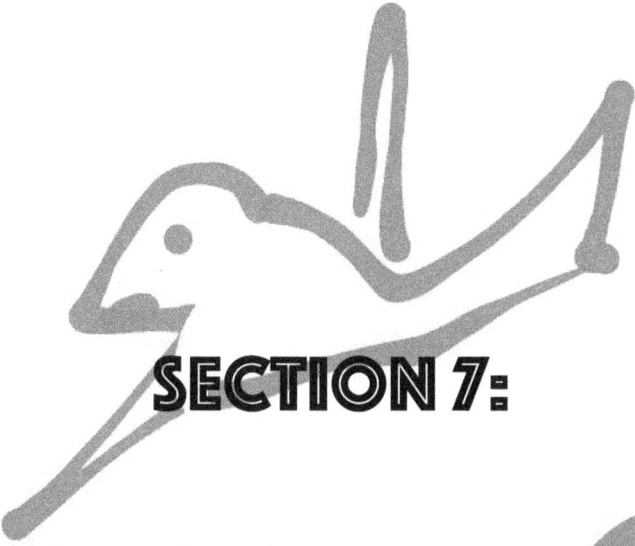

SECTION 7:

EXPLORING YOUR OWN MINDSETS

Mindsets: What Defines Me?

I think it's an interesting challenge to think about where I am now, and why and how I have the drive I have, and what defines that drive.

I remember very well something my dad told me when I was worried that I was giving my son too much autonomy. My dad and I were sitting at Donut King, drinking coffee and eating a muffins—he was munching on a raisin-bran muffin, and I was eating a carrot cake muffin, trying to convince myself that the "carrot" trumped the "cake" .... At any rate, he said something that struck me as pure gold, and it's something I'll always hold close to my heart as words of wisdom:

"The worst thing you can do is to destroy a person's drive."

How true!

In an ever-changing world, I've found that innovation has been the key to my success. I enjoy envisioning and building new products, processes, programs, and ways to do things, and I feel quite grateful to be a change agent.

Currently, I'm interested in finding new ways to help advance the productive use of technology for personal, scientific, and community development.

I've diversified myself over the years in order to be able to respond to changing times and needs, and to develop products that help people and organizations grow.

Let's start a the beginning:

Engineering and Geology: Worked as an intern and then as a technical professional. At the same time, I tried out being an entrepreneur and formed a small exploration company where I bought oil and gas leases, obtained technical information (petroleum information, seismic, etc.), and

International Operations Analyst: I worked on a master's degree in Economics and took accounting and other MBA-type courses. I started a small import-export company and represented paints and plastics products, and mixing equipment (Charles Ross and Son, Sun Chemicals, Mearl Pigments, and more). I participated in technical training and marketed the products in Bolivia, Paraguay, and other countries. In addition, I imported products from South America (Ecuador, Paraguay, Bolivia) and Africa (Kenya). I was hired by Kerr-McGee and worked as an international operations analyst in the pigments division where I worked with marketing to develop new pigment products and to estimate demand. I also helped with the planning of synthetic rutile product development (Alabama) and rutile / ilmenite mining in Australia.

International program development and marketing: I continued in international marketing and product development by leading several trade and commerce missions to Paraguay. One had to do with free trade, with an emphasis on technical products. The others had to do with educational initiatives, which included launching online courses through the Paraguayan American Cultural Center in Asuncion and prison reform and facilities reconstruction in Paraguay. At the same time, I indulged my passion for literature (and my MA and Ph.D.) by working with women writers and putting together an anthology of Paraguayan women writers, which was published in 2000. I received recognition for my work in Paraguay from the Paraguayan Labor Ministry, the Paraguayan Ministry of Navigation and Ports, the Paraguay Writer's Association, and the Paraguayan American Cultural Center.

My roles expanded and I worked at the University of Oklahoma where I lead teams to successfully compete for contracts to deliver training and knowledge exchange in Azerbaijan, Kazakhstan, Turkmenistan, Mozambique, Kenya, and other countries. The exchanges were two-way: we established learning and training centers in the countries, sent teams, and then received visiting teams at the University of Oklahoma and other locations.

Online Education: Turbulent times made many of the initiatives I had been involved with very difficult due to travel restrictions. So, in the late 1990s, after earning my Ph.D., I thought it would be fun to see just how easily we could create online learning. Granted, the first attempts were primitive, but they worked! The ideas and approaches (very basic learning management systems) caught on, and I was asked to lead teams to innovate and launch online initiatives at the University of Oklahoma's College of Liberal Studies and also the Energy Institute. I received a quite a bit of recognition for this, including Outstanding Employee several times.

Instructional Design: I obtained certificates and completed training in instructional design and online instruction, and began to help companies develop and launch their online courses and materials. I offered my services and worked for a number of textbook companies and universities as a consultant. The companies include Pearson, Cengage, McGraw-Hill, MidAmerica College, Florida State College Jacksonville, Learningmate, Troy University, and Texas A&M. I conducted extensive research and completed a number of technical manuals and books on e-learning, published by a well-known technical publisher, Packt Publishing, of Birmingham, UK.

Global teams and projects: I am very comfortable working with distributed teams, and have participated in and managed projects with teams from India, South America, China, and more. I speak and write Spanish and continue to be involved in developing events, promotion, and intellectual property transfer. I can manage teams using different products to develop digital and cloud-based products. Some elearning products include Moodle, Canvas, Blackboard, Camtasia, Articulate. The teams have included programmers who are working in C++, Ruby on Rails, and various HTML and XML editors. In terms of big data, I have worked with teams who are developing applications for integrating data across multiple platforms or evaluating patterns using new analytical approaches.

Technical Innovation: I am always looking for ways to spur outcomes-based innovation. I tend to think of my experiences in developing elearning solutions before there was much of a framework for it as some of the most exciting in my life. A close second has been looking at technical innovation and finding out about the new ways to explore for and develop oil and gas reserves (conventional and unconventional), and also to revitalize mature fields. I'm also constantly looking for emerging technologies that can help solve problems, such as dealing with produced water, cleaning up polluted water, optimizing disposal, using new digital techniques (UAS / etc.) to pinpoint environmental problems and collect data that would lead to their solutions.

Drones, Sensors, New Technologies: I am actively organizing workshops and courses on drones / UAV (unmanned aerial vehicles) that focus on new capabilities that will enable breakthrough techniques for assuring integrity of structures and early detection of problems. The scope is limited only by the imagination -- but at the same time, privacy and air safety concerns are paramount. Key in the development of new drone technology is the development of sensors that can be used in multiple applications, from drone to helicopter, regular plane, and fixed locations.

Pitchapalooza – Innovative Ventures Meet Private Capital: Think of a "Shark Tank" pitch fest, but with more funding, more ideas, and they are not simply consumer products or software apps, but also involve business plans. For example, they can have to do with the revitalization of oil fields by means of the application of oil field chemicals. The owner of the field may be undercapitalized and does not have the funds to invest. So, they may be willing to sell a 10% working interest stake in order to obtain the funds to do an updated reservoir model and then to purchase the chemicals and services of a company.

Next Steps –Taking this further: Once we have initial proof of concept and success, the key is to take it further. Where can we go with it?

Are They Really Reptilian Aliens? World Leaders Explained.

Yet another shocking behavior by a public official, and I wonder if they have any regard at all for human life.

According to InfoWars and other conspiracy theory websites, the world's powerful leaders live in the shadows, managing from behind the curtain. Some are actually in the public view, but not many. What they have in common is that none human. They are Reptilian Aliens.

I review again their behavior and I'm riveted and utterly perplexed: What were they thinking? What kind of person are they?

But, that's a line of questioning that leads me nowhere, because the answers will never crystallize into any kind of certainty. The more we delve into possible psychological explanations, the more we distance ourselves from the heart of the matter and lose ourselves in details of childhood formative events. It's a hopeless morass.

To understand world leaders, we can't focus on the individuals. And, we can't simply discount them as being from another planet (although it's a satisfying idea).

We have to look beyond the individuals making outrageous remarks or doing what used to be the unthinkable. It is necessary to take a step back and ask questions that approach the issue from different directions.

1. What are the conditions that made it possible for this type of leader or company to exist?
2. What are the societal beliefs and collectively held attitudes that actually encouraged this sort of person or company, to

the point that they were almost "willed into existence" by society.

3. What are the underlying assumptions about agency and free will? Who has power? Who gets to decide?

4. Where are there possible mischaracterizations and exaggerations in the press? Who benefits?

5. If the news generates a certain feeling in the reader, what is it? What is the first feeling you feel when you read something? Examine your own response. Fear? Desire? Anger? Hunger? Keep in mind that if any of those four emotions are triggered, you're probably working with your limbic system. It is the so-called Reptilian Brain – the "Four Fs" – Fight, Flight, Fornicate, Feed.

Which brings me to an observation: One of the more persistent conspiracy theories is that the powerful world leaders are actually "Reptilian Aliens" who live among us.

If it is true, it's interesting because the main emotions triggered by the so-called Reptilian Aliens are those primal emotions from the reptilian brain.

The leaders are not reptilian. We are. And, as such, we're easily manipulated.

Dog-Shaming: A Meme Still Going Strong, but Why??? (Okay, I'm laughing, too)

I love dogs. I thought I'd start with that disclosure so that my uncontrollable giggling when I peruse the Dog-Shaming social media site (http://www.dogshaming.com/) is not because I harbor malice for Man's Best Friend. Actually, I'm not quite sure why the little hand-written placards hung around the necks of the naughty dogs, often photographed at the scene of the crime make me smile. I am going to search my own heart and soul in an attempt to understand my rather callous attitude.

1. Naughty dog! And I repent nothing! There is something satisfying about seeing a fellow sentient being able to behave in complete freedom and express his or her inner self and satisfy needs without any shame.

Here is an example of absolutely unrepentant dogs and their behavior:

I like to wait for my owner to be painting a fine line before barking loud enough to make her jump and mess up! (I will do it again, too)

2. Unconditional love comes with a price, right? We love our dogs because they love us. They do not do things to hurt us – after all, they love us unconditionally. They just do it because it's in their nature. They're dogs!

3. Human socialization processes often involve shaming. It works on humans. It works NOT AT ALL on dogs. How many times as a child were you shamed into behaving in accordance with societal (or at least family) norms? Did you like it? I would wager that you felt as I did. You did not like it. Shaming always filled me with a terrible discomfort and a sneaking suspicion that perhaps I was not worthy.

It also made me feel on the edge of being on the edge of absolute rejection. As a part of the human pack, I know that I cannot survive completely on my own, no matter how fast the Internet connection and the number of Twitter followers I might have.

4. Schadenfreude. This is a fundamental human emotion upon seeing the misfortune of others (especially those of whom we are envious). No, it's not admirable. And, no, it's not psychologically healthy to inwardly gloat when someone rich, powerful, beautiful, famous, or privileged suffers a public exposure of some fairly trivial misfortune (gets photographed looking bloated, or their gorgeous yacht springs a leak).

5. Transgressive behavior that satisfies needs.

"I'm on the naughty list... I ate the Christmas cookies."
The dog (a black Lab?) looks satisfied.
http://www.dogshaming.com/2016/12/im-on-the-naughty-list/

6. Establishing a community of interest: other dog lovers who share frustrating experiences. We feel affirmed by knowing we are not alone.

7. Woven into the warp and woof (sorry!) of our lives. And, they are our children who never actually mature and who always seem delighted to see us when we come home after a long day – even if they've been naughty.

Mystery Solved

I've been eating cash from Mom's purse for years (7)
Mom thought she was just Irresponsible with cash.
I returned it when I was done – IN THE YARD AS POO
http://www.dogshaming.com/2016/12/mystery-solvent/

8. Who's the master here? Our dogs, our masters.

Why do you need yoga when you can run trail with me?! I'm just trying to ensure that you get lots of cardio.

http://www.dogshaming.com/2016/12/form-over-fitness-i-dont-think-so/

Requiem: Debbie Reynolds and Carrie Fisher

Debbie Reynolds

My mother and Debbie Reynolds were born in the same year, 1932, and roughly in the same region of the country. My mother was from Oklahoma, but her family had hailed from West Texas, and Debbie was born in West Texas. Debbie Reynolds had precisely the screen persona that my mother admired, and she adored dance, especially tap.

Shuffle -shuffle -ball change -ball change -shuffle -shuffle -shuffle...

The dancing of Gene Kelly in Singing in the Rain was muscular, assertive, and totally post-War "can do" and Debbie Reynolds had the kind of wholesome energy that just absolutely lit up the screen and filled you with a kind of positive glow that cheered you and made it exciting to face the day.

I can only imagine how it must have been, in those days of matinee theater, to go to a movie and see the blaze of positive energy and the happy endings on a big screen when little screens were not really an option.

My mother wanted to be like Debbie Reynolds. She had, on the face of it, a fairy tale life. She married a professional who was very successful. And yet she was haunted by anxiety, migraine headaches, and depression almost all her life, until she was diagnosed with thyroid cancer, and it became clear that perhaps the mood swings and gloomy outlook were biochemical. She was a seeker of solace, and she went to many different churches. There were many, but the ones that stood out most in my mind were

Debbie Reynolds is a screen legend. I, needless to say, never met her. I did not even see many of her films in their entirety. However, the fact my mother so admired her energy, her tap dancing, her radiantly lit wholesome screen presence, and the sensitivity that accompanied it makes me reflect on my mother. Why did my mother so gravitate to Debbie Reynolds? Why did others of her generation (and others)? I think that the answers are multiple – we all know that a Hollywood persona is in many ways a construct, and that things are not really as they appear on the screen. Certainly Debbie Reynolds's life was not all cheer and happiness. She had remarkably pitiful luck with men, at least those she married. All betrayed her in one way or another. The first, Eddie Fisher, ran off – very publicly, in fact – with Elizabeth Taylor. The others simply stole, embezzled, or otherwised destabilized to the point of wiping her out financially. But, true to one of her archetypal roles, Debbie was (or was represented to be) the absolutely Unsinkable Molly Brown, and she persevered, beyond pain and fear, to rebuild herself, her wealth, her family.

And, certainly it was not without its travails. Carrie Fisher was so troubled with bipolar disorder and drug addiction that there were times everyone feared the worst. Yet, up to the very end, Debbie had a glowing, radiant presence, and nowhere was it more evident than when she posed with her daughter, Carrie, whose ravaged face and body could not be so channeled into a single clear beam of light, but instead was like looking into the inside of a meat grinder, and all you saw was the sharp metal of life tearing her up, along with her corporeal manifestation, reduced to hamburger.

In photos of my mother, roughly contemporaneous with Debbie Reynolds's appearances in Singing in the Rain (released in 1952– but filmed year after my mother graduated from high school), Tammy and the Bachelor (1957), and many others, my mother's slim, athletic made her a perfect body double for the dancers on the big screen. Also, her unflinching enthusiasm for tennis, fishing, boating, hiking, echoed the open and unrestrained style of Debbie, both "girl next door" and the embodiment of American self-actualization.

And, where the actual origins of that self-actualization? Like my mother, Debbie Reynolds the child lived, breathed, and imbibed the unstable Depression years, where migrants from Texas and Oklahoma in California literally starved to death, but more often simply succumbed to opportunistic maladies that preyed upon the malnourished and chronically exhausted.

My mother's life was framed in outer security, but inwardly, I know for a fact she was riddled with insecurity. It manifested in her fears for her salvation and her pursuit of the ideal church (and spiritual condition).

In the case of Debbie Reynolds, I wonder if her bad choices in husbands represented a kind of traumatic re-enactment of the literal (as well as existential) instability she inhabited as a child. While her parents provided stability, she was in no way surrounded by it. The Great Depression was a time of extreme social inequality and there were few or no safety nets.

So, she introduced instability into her most stable and prosperous moments. Why? They were opportunities to survive, overcome, and be unsinkable as she capsized her own boat, and ran into icebergs of her own making, over and over and over again.

Somehow, the process is both enlightening and inspiring – regardless of agency, and who actually caused the capsizing…

Carrie Fisher
Despite all the plastic surgery, Carrie Fisher had a ravaged face, and her aura radiated suffering, even when she was on top of the world, and ripping up the angst of existence with her quick, irreverent wit.

I'm saying this from very, very arms-length. Carrie Fisher's raw honesty and open quirkiness gave people permission to be themselves and to be vulnerable. It also satisfied a universal schadenfreude upon seeing the famous brought low.

Carrie Fisher's novels were bestsellers. Would they have been so popular if they were not a thinly veiled account of the scandals and foibles of Hollywood "royalty"?

After she passed away, I went on a Carrie Fisher movie binge – well, mini-binge. I watched a number of movies and also the movie version of *Postcards from the Edge.* I enjoyed her acting. She was good. I did not like *Postcards from the Edge* as much – it was a bit of an emotional one-trick pony.

That said, now Carrie Fisher and Debbie Reynolds have been beatified. That is good. It is nice to see the narrative being shaped into one of eternal mother-daughter love and devotion. It was very touching that they lived adjoining houses, and a shared lot.

They say that death is one of the most effective rehabilitators of one's life. All is forgiven. That is, all is forgiven if you're lucky. If not, you're demonized and scandalized to be held out as a cautionary tale.

The Christmas Letter.

Okay so it's not Christmas. And no, it's not the day I thought it would be, the day I thought you'd actually tell me something that would move me and convince me that this could be real, could be sincere, could be something that takes us to that transcendent moment of unity with the divine. Sir Philip Sidney redux. Yes.

And yet how can that happen when I'm not actually where that could ever occur; I'm constantly undermining my own narrative – not for cynicism's sake, but to introduce that euphoric effervescence of the absurd, the smiling laughing joyously embracing the universe through tears through the wrenching sense of loss that I feel every time I look into your eyes…

Walk walk walk into the church. It is a quest for meaning. Yes. And so we look beyond the way that
society cut the cloth, stitched the fashion so that I'm always a half a beat awkward – ahead? Behind?

Off somewhere to the side?

I'm a fungible good. I'm absolutely replaceable. In fact, I have a infinite number of substitutes that will always always be absolutely indistinguishable from the first one. Does that mean I'm a copy?

Well, not if I came first. And, is it possible for copies to be better than the original? Actually, copies are almost always better than the original – the original can get tattered, weathered, rough around the edges. The copy can be copied fresh every day. The copy is forever young.

Take that, Bob Dylan! Forever Young? Yes, if you're a copy – a derivative not of the real, but of the simulacrum. Sound to complicated? Don't look at me! Look at the factories, the mass replication of the action of stamping out, of impressing, of imprinting something we'll be able to relate to in time and space.

And, well, that's what it's all about, isn't it? Relate to something in time and space. Tell me how it is.

Then, slow me down. Place me at your side at the scraggly beach where scrawny dogs sicken and die, and yet, in this context of paradise, I just don't know how to process their suffering. And all around, scrawny suffering couples from Canada look off to the sunset. I see dead eel on the beach. It died trying to swallow a big fish. Yup. It died. Appetite? Dreaming too large? Over-reaching – simply going for the Big Deal without actually scaling and scoping the project.

Bon Bon. What an adorable name for a lean whippet mix. Oh my dear, sweet dog. Where are you now? Bon Bon. A sweet little short-haired dog obviously in need of medicine. His owner – skinny, too - -but from a different sickness – asked me for money to pay for treatment for Bon Bon. I would have given it to him, but I did not have any money with me. Also, I thought it quite likely that whatever donation I gave toward Bon Bon would not end up there. Bon Bon would not get the antibiotics he needed. No. His master would get the heroin (or something stronger) he needed.

It was raining on Thanksgiving day. Sayulita. I love the weather when it's overcast, cool, and when we sit in the kitchen and listen to music and play dominoes. I can't believe it was more than a year ago. It was such a beautiful time – wet, heavy air, the gray clouds hanging low in the horizon, and then the hurricane outer bands started to come our way. We sat on the roof and watched the clouds spark up with light and fingers of electricity that made me wonder if you, too, had the beauty of life, light, magic, and a new mind's right inside your heart. How long will we last? What will happen? It's the fear of walking around with mismatched socks. Or is it?

Oh just tell me. And so now I can go back to my memories of that unforgettable Thanksgiving Day. I was in Sayulita, Nayarit, Mexico. We had no internet. I used the services of the local internet café to be in touch. And, we walked downtown in the drizzle for a lovely lunch. I ate a delicious marlin burrito. We sat toward the back, and the wait staff moved a big portable fan so that it blow on us and cool us down. I wanted to swim. I wanted to run on the beach. Neither possibility was an option. It was raining. And, we were monitoring the situation. A late-season hurricane was, in theory, bearing down on us. The damp chill made me reach for your hand and look into your eyes.

Ah memories. Ah life. How sweet. How ephemeral. How lovely it is to swim in a sea of tears.

****

Time passes. The time I wasted when I could have been focusing on making huge inroad, making more money. But I did well. Isn't that enough? And, I have to be honest to who I am, right? I'm more a creative thinker, beat-of-my-own drum / drummer type of person.

Dream so much like many dreams. Creatures. I was supposed to a playa lake bed. But, it was filled with molten salt and creepy salt monsters.

I can do as much as possible with automatic writing. Temps perdu. Recherchez la femme. Okay. It's something that always makes sense: Be the most distinguished Proust scholar ever.

Try to improve my accent. In English? Spanish?

****

The New Year's Letter.

It's not New Year's Day. I can say I'm looking at the Chinese New Year, and well, that would be nothing more or less than the truth. I'm eager to have this year end. It has been a weird one. I've been fortunate, but it has not felt like it. Family things were bad. But they could have been worse.

The industry has been bad. Work has been rough. But it could have been worse.

What happened last year? Good things? Bad things? Supposedly, the year of the Rooster will be a pretty good one for a Dog like me. 12 years ago was definitely good for me. It's a bit scary to think of my age. I'm so eager kick into gear and do some big things, but I look at my chronological age and I wonder if I should be doing something like kicking back and going into semi-retirement. But, I know I will have at least 15 more years of active life, and it does not make much sense to stop now, especially if I am fated to live another 30 years or more, like my dad and uncle. How do I finance that? Plus, I need to help get my son on his feet – if I do not, nothing I've done will really make much sense. I must face the fact that I will probably need him some day. But, let's say I don't. I at least need to do all I can to see that he can be self-sufficient.

It's wet outside. Supposedly it's going to get icy. That will happen later. I want to take advantage of how things are right now. I feel calm, and the office is tranquil. I am slated to play tennis tonight, but I am sure it won't happen because it will probably be too icy to get to the court. The court is a nice one, with 6 indoor courts, but it closes when the weather is bad. Do I blame them? No.

Even with all the ice, do I wish I were in a different place? Location? Do I want to live in a tropical paradise? I think that the question revolves around whether or not you think that the tropics are necessarily paradise. I think of them as snaky, buggy, persistent dampness and a pervasive scent of mildew.

That said, it's nice to not to have to feel cold, and it's good to sweat. But, so much sweating limits one's choices – footwear, clothing, and more.

If I could be a big deal in a resort town, would I do it? Would I like to be the big fish in a little pond? Honestly, there are two models that most seem to follow – build, sell or rent vacation homes is the big one. The problem with that is that you are constantly having to attract renters. Then, once they are there, you have to be a great host. That seems like work to me. Let's say you sell out to people who then rent it out and all you do is provide the services and they pay a fee. That's easier, but there's not so much profit in it. Either way, it's not very intellectually stimulating. I suppose it's engaging because you can be creative, and it's exciting to have challenges to tackle. But, I wonder if you ever actually come out ahead – you sink in a lot of money, and so you've got a lot of sunk costs. But, once you achieve cash flow are you actually earning more than you would have if you had just preserved your capital in the bank?

I don't know. I have my one experiment in that area – my "flip" house in Pawnee. So far, I've sunk about $73,000 in it. It's valued on Zillow at $89,000 but I think it's probably listable at $110,000. I don't really want to sell it, but I'm not using it at all, thanks to the winter weather and the fact that my dad has been so down.

The earthquakes are not helping property values. I'm disgusted that Erin Brockovitch decided to visit Pawnee and other sites – I know she was trying to stir up outrage and action against oil companies. I agree that we should not inject so much produced water. Good. But

– she's known for protesting toxic water. So – now the perception will be that we have earthquakes AND contaminated drinking water. Not good for property values! Grr! But, perhaps any publicity is good publicity, and it will be an opportunity to show that things are completely turned around and revitalized. It could happen! Look at the Rocky Mountain Arsenal! From SuperFund site to now oen of the coolest wildlife refuge areas in the United States. Just don't pay attention to the 9-legged frogs and the fish born with no eyes. (just joking).

5.8 earthquake, epicenter Pawnee. September. 5 days after completing my updates. So frustrating.

Well. The year of the rooster should be better. My Pawnee next door neighbor has a rooster and 10 hens. Does that bode well? Augur well?

I hope so!

Wild turkeys can fly

Wild turkeys can fly. I used to see them in the parking lot of Excelsior College in Albany, New York. They were reddish brown and black. I think they were actually part of the buzzard or vulture family because they are also considered turkey vultures. I'm not sure exactly, which ones are for eating and which ones munch down on carrion. But, it was a little disturbing to think that carrion-seekers would be hanging around the college parking lot.

Turtle Sanctuary

If I were a baby endangered turtle, a little hatchling born on the coast of the Pacific in the Mexican state of Nayarit, I would wish to be all that is divine, and not to be released with the other ordinary mortal baby turtles as they take them in buckets from the hatcheries and set them out on the sand so they can scramble to the surf. I have a hard time imagining that the sharks, barracudas, and other hungry sea creatures, would turn down that daily manna. Turtle hatchlings are delicious and highly nutritious elements of their diet.

Shark blindness

I'm not sure what those platters shaped eyes actually see. They look around and like a boiled egg from hell with globular something or another that supposedly can detect food items in the sea and attack them with brio and gusto. But, certainly shark vision must be something to be reckoned with because shark attacks are fairly common. If one is to believe all the accounts, sharks indiscriminately attack wood and plastic and paper as well as flesh and things that swim. So, one might think that the best way to protect oneself would be to blind the shark with a bright light. Or, how about putting a simply a bright shiny mirror? If the shark sees himself, will he be afraid? I do not know shark behavior and I would not to test that hypothesis with my own life. For example a surfboard with a mirrored bottom might terrify the shark and make him swim away.

Or, it could make him aggressive. Or for the more Narcissus sharks, after seeing his or her image in the mirror, the shark might simply follow and never leave you. It would be hard to have a nice surfing afternoon knowing that a shark is enchanted by his own image in the mirror that is the bottom of your surfboard.

Shark in love

Everyone knows that a shark thinks a surfboard looks like a tasty snack of seal. Things flying underneath are confusing. But, what about things flying overhead? What people may not recognize is that a flock of sea birds may cause confusion because there are too many parallels. Things flying through the sky. Things flying on the surface of the ocean. And things swimming beneath the surface. Looking up to that tasty snack of surfboards. So, we have these parallel blocks that ordinarily would not mix with each other except for the idea of a snack. So, imagine being at sleepy seaside village of Lo de Marcos in Nayarit, Mexico, on your surfboard while a person on the beach eats a tasty stack of tortillas. The sharks surge from below. The seagulls swoop down from above. Suddenly we see the parallel populations interpenetrate. All for the sake of a snack.

ABOUT THE AUTHOR

Susan has been exploring mindsets for many years, not only of different types of people, but of people in different types of circumstances. In addition to exploring their ways of viewing the world, she is interested in how they view themselves, and how their sense of self evolves and shifts over time. Her approach blends science and the humanities, as does her life, with petroleum geology blended with the study of literature, rhetoric, and writing.